115
122
140

DATE DUE

JUL 17 1993		
	JAN 0 4 2000	
	MAR 0 2 2000	
MAR 2 5 2003		
	APR 0 1 2003	
	JAN 1 4 2005	

DEMCO 38-297

Conrad's Romanticism

Conrad's Romanticism

David Thorburn

New Haven and London Yale University Press

1974

Published with assistance from
the Louis Effingham deForest Memorial Fund.

Designed by John O. C. McCrillis
and set in Baskerville type.
Printed in the United States of America by
The Vail-Ballou Press, Binghamton, N.Y.

Published in Great Britain, Europe, and Africa by
Yale University Press, Ltd., London.
Distributed in Latin America by Kaiman & Polon,
Inc., New York City; in Australasia and Southeast
Asia by John Wiley & Sons Australasia Pty. Ltd.,
Sydney; in India by UBS Publishers' Distributors Pvt.,
Ltd., Delhi; in Japan by John Weatherhill, Inc., Tokyo.

FOR MY MOTHER | AND FOR
AND FATHER | BARBARA

Contents

Preface

It is not hard to imagine Conrad's reaction to my present enterprise. He distrusted critics, though their judgments afflicted him more intensely than he would acknowledge, and he was impatient especially with terms like Realism, Romanticism, and Naturalism. Mere temporary formulas, he called them.[1] "There is even one abandoned creature," he once observed with something less than amusement, "who says I am a neo-platonist? What on earth is that?"[2]

I take these sentiments, and similar ones I've not mentioned, as an incitement to caution but not to silence. Resisting the small temptation to call Conrad a neo-Romantic, I want to focus, nonetheless, on certain qualities in his work that have come in recent years to be slighted or misunderstood.

The Conrad who emerges, or is permitted to emerge, from the thickets of recent scholarship is a modern writer first and last, profoundly "one of us," as the critics (remembering Lord Jim) are fond of saying. This Conrad is the political prophet whose insights into imperialism and revolutionary desperation constitute a text for our times;[3] he is a giant in exile, as the subtitle of one recent book has it,[4] whose acute sense of alienation measures the wintry afflictions of the modern spirit. Conrad provides us with "new myths for a profane civilization," according to another recent study.[5] Agreeing, but in his own terms, J. Hillis Miller tells us that Conrad keeps company with the "poets of reality," being a writer who follows nihilism to the very heart of its darkness and "so prepares the way beyond it"[6]—a road not taken, apparently, by Auden or Frost (neither of whom is mentioned in Miller's account) but traveled decisively by five other poets of this century:

Yeats, Eliot, Dylan Thomas, Stevens, and William Carlos
Williams.

With a few important exceptions, the habit—or perhaps the need—of modern criticism has been to retrieve
Conrad from the century in which he lived more than
half his life and in which he published not only his two
apprentice novels, *Almayer's Folly* (1895) and *An Outcast
of the Islands* (1896), but also, among other and lesser
things, *The Nigger of the "Narcissus"* (1898), "Youth"
(1898), *Heart of Darkness* (1899), and a substantial part of
Lord Jim, which began to appear serially in *Blackwood's
Magazine* in October 1899 and was published complete in
1900. That this rescue operation has increased our understanding of Conrad's achievement cannot be disputed. But
as any Wordsworthian, not to say Freudian, knows, even
the most loving eye half-creates the objects it perceives;
and this seems to me clearly true of the purposeful, high-
minded ardor with which modern scholarship has em-
braced Conrad.

The account of Conrad provided in the following pages
questions this impulse to transform the author of *Typhoon* into an image of ourselves. My argument is
revisionist, even in a sense conservative, and emphasizes
Conrad's affinities with the *fin-de-siècle* tradition of the
adventure story and, ultimately, with the Romantic poets.
In his very subjects and in his dominant attitudes toward
those subjects, I want to suggest, Conrad was in fundamental ways a man of the nineteenth century, and his affinities with Wordsworth especially are even stronger and
more decisive than his connection with, say, Kafka and
other prophets of our disorder. To say this is not entirely
to deny Conrad's modernity but to qualify it by making
two related assertions which it will be part of my purpose
to try to justify: first, that Conrad habitually relied on
what must be called Romantic modes of storytelling and

created fictional worlds in which alienation, despair, and human separateness are contained, however precariously, by a stoic Romanticism grounded in a sense of human sharing and continuity; and second, that the increasingly powerful argument for Romanticism itself as a modern tradition—the phrase is Robert Langbaum's—receives convincing, perhaps crucial support from Conrad's example.

Indeed, I would align my approach to Conrad, and to early twentieth-century fiction generally, with a good deal of the scholarship concerning Romanticism that has emerged in the past two decades. The best of this work, it seems to me, is simultaneously engaged in retrieving the Romantics from New Critical neglect and in challenging the once widespread notion that Romanticism and modernism are discontinuous. My own claims for Conrad— and my brief suggestions in the epilogue concerning the major English novelists who succeeded him—are consistent in many respects with this larger enterprise of Romantic studies, and can be seen as a preliminary effort to locate modern fiction within a territory already mapped out for modern poetry.

Although I intend my title, and portions of my argument as well, to rest explicitly on this body of scholarship, I have refrained from entering directly into the fascinating continuing debate concerning the nature of Romanticism. I can see how this strategy might be questioned, since even the Romanticists disagree about the exact contours of their subject and since those whose specialties lie elsewhere may grow impatient with my use of a term that is defined only implicitly and incompletely. But I believe my reticence is defensible and even essential. First, because my primary concern is with Conrad himself, I should like to think that my account of his struggle with the materials of his life and temperament would remain credible even for a reader suspicious of the expansionist understanding of Romanticism I quite obviously accept. Second, I am confident that despite differences in emphasis and even in substance, there remains a genuine consensus concerning the essential features of Romanticism. So widespread is this agreement, indeed, that I have felt it unnecessary to spend much time talking about Conrad's escapist tendencies, his exoticism, his neo-primitivism. Further, the aspects of his work on which I do focus—his preoccupation with the drama of maturation, his richly elegiac interest in "things far distant and men who have lived," his intensive self-reflexiveness—all this is so commonly understood to characterize those writers everyone agrees to call Romantic that it would seem supererogatory to offer yet another systematic definition.

I do not, of course, imagine that the Conrad described in this book is an exact counterpart of Wordsworth, although I do want to insist on their important resemblances. Nor do I think my argument is significantly disturbed by the fact that Conrad's fiction is largely innocent of that visionary strain in Romanticism whose chief exponent and scholar is Harold Bloom. I think Bloom is overly preoccupied with Blake, and I am scarcely alone in resisting his excessive emphasis on the prophetic and the apocalyptic.[7] But the more important—and less contentious—assumption of my argument is simply that the visionary side of Romanticism survives but feebly after Shelley. If it is clear that earlier scholars erred or at least simplified in their restrictive definitions, it remains true that Romanticism's journey into our own century was a complex and endangered one, in which the heroically self-searching enterprise of the first Romantics was absorbed by a culture which inevitably domesticated and attenuated their pioneer vigor. I think this trivializing and reductive impulse remains characteristic of our literary culture even today and that Blake's vision of "the real man, the Imagination" is not its only casualty. From this perspective certain early modern writers may be said to play exemplary redemptive and mediating roles, the shape of their careers suggesting an unsolemn Spenserian fable wherein the Damsel Romanticism is sustained and nourished by various writers through the nineteenth century but is captured finally, and betrayed, by two sibling dragons—a Pre-Raphaelite and Rider Haggard. The damsel is rescued and restored to a semblance of her first beauty by two knights, Conrad and Yeats. Conrad, of course, slays Rider Haggard; and Yeats, after a struggle, slays Christina Rossetti.

I remain enough of a formalist to feel some slight embarrassment at the fact that the view of Conrad urged in these pages is more congruent with Conrad's own explanations for his work than the view that is implicit in many of the best-known commentaries, whose emphasis on the solitariness of Conrad's characters, the existential darkness of his fictional world, seems to me not so much wrong as one-sided or partial. Yet there is warrant for my perspective not only (as I hope to show) in the texts themselves but also in the work of a minority of Conrad's critics: in some of his contemporary reviewers and, more notably, in the writings of Ian Watt and the late Morton Zabel.

When I began this study I was concerned less with Conrad's place in literary history than with the problem of his unevenness as a writer, but I came finally to realize that to account for Conrad's puzzling failures was also, and inescapably, to confront the insistently Romantic character of his work. The conventional explanation for Conrad's decline, an explanation elaborated on Freudian lines in Thomas Moser's important book, sees the later works as departures in which the austere pessimism of the major novels and stories yields to easy affirmation in books like

Chance or *The Rover*.[8] I am in sympathy with much in Moser's argument, but also feel that his sharp distinction between early and late Conrad needs qualification. My own emphasis on the continuities in Conrad's work tries to supply such qualification, tries to render the arc of his career more intelligible by calling attention to themes and to particular dramatic scenes which preoccupy him continually and which find expression in his undervalued autobiographical books as well as his fiction. This emphasis leads me to explain Conrad's later failures somewhat differently, as a return in part to the debased Romantic mode of the Stevensonian adventure story—the mode to which Conrad's earliest fiction largely belongs, and also the mode whose conventions and assumptions are central even in his finest work.

My argument thus requires that I spend time with some of the lesser works, and particularly with *Romance,* Conrad's little-read collaboration with Ford Madox Ford. Great writers may quicken us to reverence for many reasons, one of the best being that they are capable of writing very badly. In this, too, Wordsworth stands with Conrad like a brother.

D. T.

New Haven, Connecticut
June 1973

Acknowledgments

Because acknowledging one's intellectual debts has become a scholarly convention of such wide usage the obligations I record here will inevitably seem less substantial than they really are. I can only protest, not overcome, this state of affairs.

Merle Spiegel began this project as my editor and became my close friend before her work was done. I am grateful to her for unmeasurable aid and comfort. For inspiriting discussions concerning many aspects of my subject I owe a great deal to the candor and acuteness of Leo Braudy, Howard Felperin, A. B. Giamatti, Geoffrey Hartman, David Minter, and Ivo Vidan.

I have an even more extensive debt to the following friends, who read part or all of this book in manuscript and whose generous suggestions made it better: A. Walton Litz, Richard M. Ludwig, Thomas Moser, Robert Pinsky, Martin Price, Barbara Thorburn, and Alan Trachtenberg.

For the last ten years Albert J. Guerard and Ian Watt have honored me with their rigorous criticism, encouragement, and friendship. They have affected this book, of course, and my sense of vocation as a teacher and critic. But what I owe them has other, larger dimensions.

Portions of this book were published in somewhat different form in my essay on Conrad in *Romanticism: Vistas, Instances, Continuities,* ed. David Thorburn and Geoffrey Hartman (Cornell University Press, 1973). I am grateful to the publishers for permission to reprint.

For permission to quote from the manuscript of *Romance* and from Conrad's unpublished letters to Ford

Madox Ford, I am obliged to the Beinecke Rare Book and Manuscript Library at Yale University. It is a pleasure to record my special thanks to Marjorie G. Wynne, Research Librarian at the Beinecke, for her unfailing helpfulness.

A Note on Texts. All my citations from Conrad's work refer to the *Collected Edition of the Works of Joseph Conrad,* 21 volumes (London: J. M. Dent and Sons, 1946–55). Pagination in this edition is identical with the Dent Uniform Edition (1923–28) and with the Canterbury Edition (Garden City, N.Y.: Doubleday, Page and Company, 1924–26).

Conrad's Romanticism

1   Bearings

"Do try to keep the damned sea out if you can," Conrad wrote in the margin of the first draft of a critical essay on his work. "My interests are terrestrial after all." [1] And in the letters of his last years, Conrad consistently minimizes the importance of setting in his fiction: "I have always tried to counteract the danger of precise classification, either in the realm of exoticism or of the sea." [2] The force of Conrad's desire to elude such easy labels is revealed with poignant clarity in his author's notes and also, I think, in Richard Curle's account of a meeting between Conrad and the Dean of Canterbury. To this distinguished cleric's friendly suggestion that he might use the Kentish countryside as the background for one of his novels, Conrad responded with indecorous and highly uncharacteristic abruptness: "I am not a topographical writer." [3]

It is impossible not to feel sympathetic toward Conrad's insistence on the seriousness of his work, and we must, although with important reservations, agree with F. R. Leavis when he writes that "Conrad had very good reason for protesting against the way in which he was placed and known as a writer about the sea." [4] But in our day, and despite Leavis's engaging ill-temper on this question, there is no danger that Conrad will be so simply misjudged.

Yet if it has now become fashionable to smile with condescending tolerance at the anonymous reviewer of *Almayer's Folly* who predicted that Conrad "might become the Kipling of the Malay Archipelago," [5] how are we to respond when a serious contemporary critic points out that the *Narcissus*'s "deadly plunge . . . on to her *port*

side" is vitally significant because port is "the left, or sinis-
ter, side"? Or when the same writer, chastizing Conrad for
failing to make "any admission of cabalistic intent" in
The Nigger of the "Narcissus," expresses disappointment
because "Conrad overloaded his mundane treatment of
the crew"? [6] For another modern commentator the same
novel "unavoidably" recalls the story of the fallen angels:
"Captain Allistoun and the officers, Baker and Creighton,
suggest God and His loyal angelic entourage; their ini-
tials, A, B, C, point to the beginning of things." [7] (But
what can we do, then, with *D*onkin?) Surely a fair-minded
reader will find these excesses less helpful than the limited
but at least accurate opinion of the reviewer who wrote in
1898: "It does not seem too much to say that Mr. Conrad
has in this book introduced us to the British merchant
seaman, as Rudyard Kipling introduced us to the British
soldier." [8] I reveal my conservative tendencies, and anticipate part of my argument, when I admit that this seems to
me a just description of one of Conrad's fundamental am-
bitions as a writer, and also that it is high praise.

Whatever else one can say about the state of Conrad
scholarship today, it is beyond dispute that Conrad has
been freed of "that infernal tail of ships" to which he objected so strenuously.[9] And if the perceptions of Conrad's
modern interpreters have entirely counterbalanced the
emphasis his reviewers placed on the exotic surfaces of his
fiction, this genuine advance has not been without cost.

It is more difficult now to conceive of Conrad in his historical context, a writer in the line of Marryat and Stevenson and Kipling whose exotic tales have much to tell us
about the infirmities but also the resilience of the Romantic imagination at a century's distance from its original
English flowering in Blake and Wordsworth. And for all
its energy and passion, modern criticism of Conrad has for

the most part remained strangely selective, has been disinclined to attend closely to Conrad's autobiographical books, to his prefaces and collected essays, to his lesser fiction. After more than two decades of intensive collective scholaring, Conrad's corpus remains something of a puzzle, an achievement of startling unevenness and, even, apparent discontinuity. Intent on establishing Conrad's claim to seriousness—"seriousness" being all too often indistinguishable from "modernity"—the critics of our time have tended to ignore or at best to minimize what Conrad's reviewers understood to be crucial: that the author of *Lord Jim* had a great deal in common with Robert Louis Stevenson.

This neglected side of Conrad's work is my root subject. In one sense, my argument is an attempt to renew and to enlarge upon the characteristic emphasis of the best contemporary reviews of Conrad's early fiction. In these articles—they are a clear minority, but more numerous than most of today's Conradians may imagine—Conrad's exotic settings receive considerable attention, and his reliance on the conventional elements of the adventure story is much discussed. But in addition, these reviews are fully aware of the distance between Conrad's fiction and that of inferior writers who work wholly within the popular genres. By implication, and somewhat haltingly, these reviews engage the question that I too want to ask and begin to answer: how does Conrad, using the very conventions and forms of the typical adventure story, wrest significance and seriousness from them?

That Conrad's most intelligent reviewers were aware of this question is clear, for example, in the May 2, 1903, issue of *The Athenaeum* where *Typhoon* and Rider Haggard's *Pearl-Maiden* are reviewed on the same page. "We are glad," the anonymous reviewer says in his lengthy *Ty-*

phoon article, "to welcome a new book by Mr. Conrad, for he is one of the few who never write without having something to say, and who never fail to say that something with the most scrupulous care." The remainder of the notice praises all four stories in the volume and singles out *Typhoon* for special commendation: "Anything more thorough and convincing of its kind we have never read." Yet despite its emphasis on Conrad's pictorial effects, the review is conscious of his psychological dimension. Amid his scene-painting, the article says, "the author never for a moment neglects his primary work, the representation of the action of the human mind and character under the influence of natural forces."

Rider Haggard, in contrast, is treated in a single cursory paragraph; he is "essentially a writer of action . . . ; a battle, a duel or a hunting scene flows readily enough from his pen, but his dialogue is . . . apt to be stilted and unreal, and his attempts to develop character . . . are not convincing." His novel, the review concludes, is "a good story for young people." [10]

A similar recognition of Conrad's distinction, but also of his kinship with writers of local color and adventure fiction, is the substance of an especially perceptive article in *The Academy* for the same year. In this piece Conrad's seriousness as a writer of sea narratives is said to put him in the company of Melville, and although the essay rightly emphasizes Conrad's desire to evoke the very flavor and atmosphere of the seafaring life, it stresses equally the fullness and profundity of his sense of character:

> Against this background [of the sea] move his characters —characters most faithfully observed, alive, full of nerve, or smitten down by the fear of sudden and awful death. We never question the truth of Mr. Conrad's characters. We may sometimes dislike his method, we may find fault with his construction, but the essential human element of

his dramas stands beyond cavil. In a word, his psychology
has the accuracy of brilliant diagnosis.[11]

Sentiments like these had become if not commonplace
at least unsurprising by 1903.[12] But even from the beginning of his career an intelligent few among the reviewers
had described Conrad as a writer who used conventional
subjects and settings in a serious, unique way. The London
Saturday Review, for example, reviewed Conrad's first
novel along with *Windabyne* by George Ranken and *Sin-
ners Twain* by John Mackie, remarking without hesita-
tion that although "all three of these books may be spoken
of as 'local colour' stories," only *Almayer's Folly* may be
"regarded seriously as a work of art." [13]

In the following year the same periodical published a
review of *An Outcast of the Islands* which enlarged on the
distinction between Conrad and the merely conventional
writers of exotic adventure. As Conrad later discovered,
this article had been written by H. G. Wells; [14] and it is
scarcely unalloyed praise. Wells is very harsh on Conrad's
prose: "His sentences are not unities, they are multitudi-
nous tandems, and he has still to learn the great half of his
art, the art of leaving things unwritten." But his praise is
at least as strong: he judges *An Outcast* to be "the finest
piece of fiction that has been published this year, as 'Almayer's Folly' was one of the finest that was published in
1895." And he has the highest regard for Conrad's grasp of
character and for his seriousness in a fictional mode
usually tainted by the trivial and the artificial:

> It is hard to understand how the respectable young gen-
> tlemen from the Universities who are engaged in cutting
> out cheaper imitations of the work of Mr. Stanley Wey-
> man and Mr. Anthony Hope can read a book like this
> and continue in that industry. Think of the respectable
> young gentleman from the University, arrayed in his sis-

ter's hat, fichu . . . and cycling gauntlets, flourishing her
hat-pin, and pretending, in deference to the supposed re-
quirements of Mr. Mudie's public, to be the deuce and all
of a taverning mediaeval blade, and compare him with
Willems the Outcast. How that reeling swaggerer lives!
    Then compare Mr. Conrad's wonderful Aissa with the
various combinations of Mr. Hope's "Duchess" and Mr.
Weyman's fitful lady that do duty in contemporary romance. How she lives and breathes . . . ! [15]

The modern impatience with Conrad's reviewers is not,
of course, entirely unjustified. Articles like those just cited
were the exception, especially in Conrad's earliest writing
years, and the majority of his reviewers during this early
period tended to emphasize the adventure and local color
in his work to the exclusion of everything else. If he was
praised, it was because his books were set in strange lands
and because their plots resembled those of the typical adventure yarn. *The Athenaeum,* for example, reviewed
Lord Jim along with a number of other novels under the
general heading "Tales of Adventure." And one imagines
that Conrad found little to choose between the reviewer's
objections to the "mannerism" of his style and his praise:

He has written nothing so good as *Lord Jim.*
    It deals with the history of a fine young officer of the
British Merchant Marine, with his ill fortune, with his de-
termination to overcome his troubles, and his singular
sensitiveness of character. It is a story of the Indian Ocean
and the Pacific written by a remarkable hand.[16]

If the notices were explicitly unfriendly, it was clearly
because Conrad's narrative strategies and psychological interests tried the patience of readers in search of good
manly adventure stories. Though untypical in its aggressive hostility (most of the reviews I have seen are more

cautious), the following article on *An Outcast of the Islands* seems nonetheless an accurate guide to the response Conrad elicited from his less intelligent reviewers and perhaps also from the public which for so long refused to buy his books. This article is especially valuable as a historical document because its assumptions concerning the exotic adventure story as a literary kind are so near the surface:

> When Mr. Conrad's former book, *Almayer's Folly,* appeared an enthusiastic critic seems to have declared that he might become "the Kipling of the Malay Archipelago." Judging by *An Outcast of the Islands* we fear that this prophesy has not been fulfilled. Mr. Kipling is a master of rapid delineation of character, of vivid directness of style. He excels in the short story because he can put into a small compass an amount of incident which, with lesser men, suffices for a whole volume. Mr. Conrad, on the contrary, is diffuse. He spreads his story over a wilderness of chapters and pages. Instead of the few vivid touches with which Mr. Kipling paints a scene, his narrative wanders aimlessly through seas of trivial detail. It is a pity, for Mr. Conrad is evidently equipped with a very thorough knowledge of the scenes which he describes and at times, when he resists his besetting sin of wordiness, he can be extremely effective. The opening scenes of this book, for example, . . . are good. But later on he seems to lose grip of his subject. The story melts among a desert of words, and the desert alas is dry. . . . Mr. Conrad does not possess Mr. Kipling's extraordinary faculty of making his natives interesting. We are sorry not to be able to write more appreciatively of what is evidently a careful and conscientious piece of work, but as it stands, *An Outcast of the Islands* is undeniably dull. It is like one of Mr. Stevenson's South Sea stories, grown miraculously long and miraculously tedious. There is no crispness about it and the action is not quick enough, a serious charge to make

against a book of adventure. Even schoolboys will probably have some difficulty in getting through it and we fear
adults will find it impossible.[17]

These representative complaints are more succinctly
embodied in this admission by a reviewer of *Almayer's
Folly:* "A feeling of disappointment that what promises to
be a tale of sturdy adventure in an unfamiliar and picturesque world, should turn into a long-drawn story of despair, is natural enough." [18]

Poor Conrad! His refusal to satisfy popular expectations
disappointed many of his contemporaries, while the conventional elements of adventure in his work, however
transformed, are ignored or minimized by many of his
modern interpreters.[19]

The modern attitude, it must be said, seems to have
some warrant in Conrad's own statements. Once, examin-
ing a Norwegian translation of one of his books, Conrad
complained about its luridly illustrated cover and said with
annoyance, "These people seem to think I am a sort of
Jack London." Though he had intelligent foreign critics
during his lifetime, Curle reports that "it was galling to
[Conrad] . . . to think that many people who read him in
translations regarded him as a blood-and-thunder writer
of adventure stories, while accepting with solemn approval some quite inferior writers." [20]

But like Conrad's assertions regarding the relative un-
importance of the sea in his novels—"I do wish all those
ships of mine were given a rest" [21]—these remarks have
far less relevance today than they did, perhaps, when Conrad made them. There is no longer any danger that Conrad will be confused with Rider Haggard. (And whatever
Conrad himself may have felt, that danger was always minimal.) But there does seem to be a real danger that important aspects of his work will be disregarded, even denied,
by a critical temper reluctant to admit that a humble and

in our day perhaps compromised fictional mode has much
to tell us about Conrad's attitudes, themes, characters,
methods.

To focus on the similarities between Conrad's work and
exotic adventure fiction is to draw attention to the fact
that there are in his books profound impulses toward the
very weaknesses whose presence in the work of inferior ro-
mancers inspired H. G. Wells's contempt when he reviewed *An Outcast of the Islands.* For the unsympathetic
reader, indeed, these impulses occasion dismay:

> One word comes before long to haunt the mind of any
> persistent reader of Conrad's stories—the word "melo-
> drama." Why does he do it? What has he got against ordi-
> nary human life? What is the purpose of all these feuds,
> assassinations, revolutionary plottings, these fearful disas-
> ters and betrayals? . . . [One must recognize an] over-
> simple pattern, disguised though it is with philosophic
> musings and moral reflections, which gives to so much of
> Conrad's work a sense of schoolboy limitations, of being
> written within a series of conventions by which in fact hu-
> man beings do not live. Even the betrayals tend to be
> breaches of a code, the result of artificial dilemmas of
> "honour" rather than acts of villainy or baseness.[22]

These remarks are limited to the short fiction. And I
think we can in general concede that there are stories in
the canon more insistently melodramatic than any of the
novels. But this must be a severely qualified concession,
for the novels—and not merely the novels of Conrad's last
years—certainly partake overgenerously of melodrama.
Everyone who has written on Conrad's Malayan phase has
remarked the way in which lush landscape seems to
awaken an even more intense lushness in Conrad's prose.
And of course this is perfectly, if lamentably, so; Albert
Guerard, speaking of the grandiloquence which so dam-

ages "The Lagoon," goes on to draw the relevant conclusion when he observes that "the true Conradian style was, like certain other great styles, achieved through the disciplining of initial excess." [23]

Agreed. And what is more, this process of disciplining or controlling excess seems to me to extend a good distance beyond the single problem of overly lush prose—seems, in fact, to involve for Conrad *all* the elements that comprise fictional narrative. For Conrad, as I think is clear beyond question, was as prone to extravagance in his plotting as he was in his language, was as likely either through simplification or exaggeration to undermine our belief in the truth of his characters' motives and emotions as to drench us in irrelevant scene painting.

Moreover, these dangers do not disappear from the work of Conrad's great period. Though muted and for the most part controlled, they insistently present themselves, more as ominous threat than as actual failure, in nearly every line Conrad wrote. The "raw material" of most serious fiction—that great lump of setting, character, circumstance, general atmosphere, whatever—which writers mold into works of art is no doubt relatively uninteresting in its original shape. At best it is merely inert, entirely dependent on the imaginative energy of the artist to bring out, to create, its life and substance. (One thinks, for example, of the drawing room anecdotes that became James's great novels.) But with writers who find their subjects in the exotic and the adventurous—in settings that are primitive, bare of restraint, demanding extremes of human response—with such writers and such subjects the initial situation is even more unpromising. For the raw material of such a writer is not simply boring or quietly inert but inherently and positively dangerous; it constitutes a pressing *active* threat to the seriousness and integrity of his work. Such material, as Morton Zabel has written, "encourages artifice":

It easily trades in mere shock and extravagance. It invites
fancy and allegory at the risk of divorcing a writer from
his native roots and ties in actual life. Despite the liberation it promises the fact-shackled spirit or the opportunities it gives the imagination, it also encourages irresponsi-
bility and triviality.[24]

It is to such risks precisely that Conrad's insistent use of
exotic and adventure material commits him: his fiction is
imperiled by its subject matter.

Conrad was entirely accurate when, in perhaps the most
moving and important letter he ever wrote, he told William Blackwood that his fiction

in its essence . . . is action (strange as this affirmation
may sound at the present time) nothing but action—
action observed, felt and interpreted with an absolute
truth to my sensations . . . action of human beings that
will bleed to a prick, and are moving in a visible world.[25]

The danger in Conrad, *Chance* included, is never too much
method but too much matter; the danger, to put it another
way, is that his people will bleed *too* much or his world
become *too* visible. For in fiction whose fundamental
materials are wars, revolutions, extremes of violence, mur-
der, suicide, heroic self-immolation—and in fiction whose
central figures are tested against these extravagant possibilities—the pressures exerted on a writer's *manner,* on *how*
he deals with his material, are incalculably intense. So that
for Conrad, more decisively, even, than for Henry James,
technique is salvation.

If the essential character of his subject matter threatened
the integrity of his art, Conrad's temperament, or at least
one aspect of that complex temperament, tended to reinforce this danger. A man whose Polish heritage celebrated
a tradition of almost medieval chivalry and whose experiences as a seaman in exotic parts of the world fitted into an

uneasy but real accord with that chivalrous tradition,
Conrad was, in his own words, a strange "concoction": "a
Polish nobleman, cased in British tar!" [26] Many of his attitudes and responses were in some degree old-fashioned,
even positively chivalric. Though deriving from sources
more personal and more respectable than the basic attitudes
of the writers of boys' adventure fiction, Conrad's assumptions about experience and his response to it in part resembled those of such writers: he tended to see life as a
perilous, exciting adventure full of decisive challenges and
testings; he tended to celebrate, both in his life and in his
writings, ideals of honor and martial valor; he tended, too,
despite his own commitment to the writing of fiction, to
revere the active life and to condemn or suspect the hesitations of intellect; he exhibited throughout his writing a
lack of interest in (and an occasional contempt for) life in
modern society, usually finding his deepest and best stories
in primitive, "uncivilized" settings. The unnamed narrator who appears briefly in the early sections of *Victory*
speaks for the Conrad I am describing:

> Nobody amongst us had any interest in men who
> went home. They were all right; they did not count any
> more. Going to Europe was nearly as final as going to
> Heaven. It removed a man from the world of hazard and
> adventure. [p. 23]

That world of hazard and adventure which Conrad
dramatized repeatedly in his writings was also the world
in which Conrad the seaman had actually lived for many
years. And although in one of his prefaces Conrad admitted that "my life as a matter of fact was far from being adventurous in itself" (*Within the Tides*, p. v), his autobiographical writing, no less than the fiction which we know
derived directly from his personal experiences, reveals
with great clarity that facet of temperament which links

him with the authors of boys' adventure tales—reveals, in short, a romanticizing impulse, a tendency to discover glamor and excitement and heroic possibilities even in surroundings like those of the merchant service, where the dullness of routine dominates life. "The romantic feeling of reality was in me an inborn faculty" (*Tides,* p. v), Conrad wrote in 1920.

Although to account completely for this strain in Conrad's temperament would no doubt be an impossible task, we may be quite certain that his Polish heritage is a decisive factor. Conrad's family were members of the *szlachta,* or landowning nobility. According to the Polish scholar Zdzislaw Najder, this nobility was "the reigning cultural force" in the Poland of Conrad's boyhood:

> The *bourgeois* element was to become more active only in the eighteen-seventies. The life of the nation was therefore dominated by the values now commonly called "soldierly" and "aristocratic," descending from the medieval ideals of chivalry. The material values of wealth and economic progress were pursued, if at all, rather shamefacedly and disregarded for the sake of more lofty and adventurous ideals of honour and duty; not a merchant or an industrialist but a soldier was held to be an example to follow.[27]

Surely it is easy to perceive variations on these ideals of honor and duty in the worst of Conrad as well as the best.

If the chivalrous tradition out of which Conrad came molded his responses, it is also true that Conrad was naturally disposed to find such a tradition congenial. It has long been a commonplace to speak of Conrad's adventurous disposition, and there is no need to consider this subject in detail. It is almost sufficient to say that the facts of his sailing life, and his way of speaking about that life after he had retired to the shore, justify Jean-Aubry's breathless rhetoric, of which this is a fair sample:

> Fate had played into the hands of the young Conrad. He had been thirsty for adventure, and now, though he was not twenty years old, he was embarking on the last romantic dynastic enterprise of the Nineteenth Century.[28]

That recent scholarship has discovered major inconsistencies in Conrad's accounts of the gunrunning episode to which Aubry is referring in this passage seems finally of less importance than the simple fact that Conrad told such a story of himself and that something resembling it almost surely did occur, if in less perilous circumstances than Conrad claims.[29] The young Carlist smuggler is, in any case, consistent with Conrad's other incarnations. He is consistent with the landlocked Polish student who longed to go to sea and who, refusing the arguments of his tutor, was finally told in exasperation, "You are an incorrigible, hopeless Don Quixote. That's what you are" (*A Personal Record,* p. 44).

He is consistent with the nine-year-old boy—and, more significantly, with the older, worldly novelist who remembered so affectionately that youthful time that he wrote of the same episode in three separate books—who wished for adventure and who, unlike other childhood dreamers, enacted his youthful fantasies in reality when he grew up:

> Only once did that enthusiasm [for geography] expose me to the derision of my schoolboy chums. One day, putting my finger on a spot in the very middle of the then white heart of Africa, I declared that some day I would go there. My chums' chaffing was perfectly justifiable. . . . Yet it is a fact that, about eighteen years afterwards, a wretched little stern-wheel steamboat I commanded lay moored to the banks of an African river.[30]

He is consistent, too, with the thirty-one-year-old sea captain, no youth now, whose ship was loading in Sydney for a trip to Mauritius:

> One day, all of a sudden, all the deep-lying historic sense
> of the exploring adventures in the Pacific surged up to
> the surface of my being. Almost without reflection I sat
> down and wrote a letter to my owners suggesting that, in-
> stead of the usual southern route, I should take the ship
> to Mauritius by way of Torres Strait.

When his owners accept the proposal, Conrad feels
qualms because the passage is a dangerous one and because

> I had not been scrupulously honest in my argumentation.
> . . . [But] I won't pretend that I regret my lapse from
> strict honesty, for what would the memory of my sea life
> have been for me if it had not included a passage through
> Torres Strait . . . along the track of the early naviga-
> tors. ["Geography and Some Explorers," *Last Essays,* pp.
> 18–19]

The quixotic Polish boy is consistent also with the romantic ship's officer who so impressed Galsworthy in 1893:

> The first mate is a Pole called Conrad and is a capital
> chap, though queer to look at; he is a man of travel and
> experience in many parts of the world, and has a fund of
> yarns on which I draw freely. He has been right up the
> Congo and all around Malacca and Borneo and other out
> of the way parts, to say nothing of a little smuggling in
> the days of his youth.[31]

Again, the adventure-hungry child can logically become
the groaning, self-dramatizing Conrad of the letters to
Marguerite Poradowska, Garnett, Meldrum, and other literary friends.[32]

The Polish aristocrat with an inborn "romantic feeling
of reality" and an adventurous past whom Galsworthy remembered made a very clear impression on Conrad's
other friends as well. Indeed, this important aspect of
Conrad's personality seems rather more obvious in the ac-

counts of Conrad the man than one might guess from a
reading of the fiction. When two men of such diverging
literary and personal styles as H. G. Wells and Ford
Madox Ford give accounts of Conrad that seem in important respects complementary, it is a safe assumption that
their common impression is highly accurate. In any case,
the Conrad of Ford's various portraits—an "Elizabethan
Gentleman Adventurer," "dark, black-bearded, passionate
in the extreme" [33]—more than resembles the Conrad described by a far less sympathetic H. G. Wells. Recalling
their first meeting, Wells notes that Conrad "talked with
me mostly of adventure and dangers, Hueffer talked criticism and style and words." [34] Conrad impressed Wells, as
he impressed everyone who later wrote about him, with
his distinct foreignness, with a politeness that was more
ornate than his most mannered and self-conscious prose,
with the "nautical trimness of his costume." The man
Wells describes sounds like an unsuccessful character from
a Conrad novel: "I found . . . something . . . ridiculous
in Conrad's *persona* of a romantic adventurous unmercen-
ary intensely artistic European gentleman carrying an exquisite code of unblemished honour through a universe of
baseness." Wells believed that Conrad once came near to
challenging Bernard Shaw to a duel because of some obscure insult Shaw had directed at Conrad's books. Wells
also reports that Conrad once urged Ford to challenge
him:

> If Conrad had had his way, either Hueffer's blood or
> mine would have reddened Dymchurch sands. I thought
> an article Hueffer had written . . . was undignified and I
> said that he had written it as if he were a discharged valet
> . . . Hueffer came over to tell me about it. "I tried to ex-
> plain to [Conrad] . . . that duelling isn't done," said
> Hueffer.

Jocelyn Baines may be right to cast doubt on this anecdote in view of Ford's reputation for exaggeration and invention,[35] but whether true to the facts or not the story
accords with the impression Conrad made on virtually
everyone. As Ford might say, it is true even if it didn't
happen.

Conrad, in any event, would hardly be deeply offended
if he were to learn of this anecdote. He seemed in fact almost eager to have his friends and family believe that the
duel M. George fights in *The Arrow of Gold* really happened, and that it happened to him.[36] In his author's note
to the book he openly states that the story is autobiographical (pp. viii–ix); he clearly implies the same thing
in letters to Colvin; and his inscription in Curle's edition
of the novel is even more explicit: "All the personages are
authentic and the facts are as stated." [37]

In other respects, too, Curle's Conrad retains the essential characteristics noted by men like Wells and Ford.
Though older in Curle's portrait, somewhat paternal toward his young friend, and of course world-famous, this
Conrad has preserved the "grand manner" and the courtli-
ness; this older Conrad exhibits, too, a "nice" sense of
honor and, with what seems to Curle a sort of heroic old-
fashionedness, believes "in the great qualities, such as
honour, loyalty, endurance, and courage." [38]

The elderly writer who was committed to these virtues
accords well enough with the younger man who responded like this to one of Garnett's anecdotes: "Yes, dear
Edward. But have you ever had to keep an enraged negro
armed with a razor from coming aboard, along a ten-inch
plank, and drive him back to the wharf with only a short
stick in your hands?" [39]

It is hardly surprising that a man with such a past, remembered by friends in such consistent postures, should

find the conventions of the adventure story congenial. Nor
is it surprising that such a man should tend toward a
vision of life in which violent and decisive eruptions are
commonplace. The good-humored impatience with moral
nuance revealed in this remark to Garnett implies the
Conrad whose letters occasionally express contempt not
only for himself but also for the profession of letters; and
it implies the Conrad of works like "Freya of the Seven
Isles" and "The Planter of Malata," stories which radically simplify human motives and have little patience
with the gossamer complexities of the moral life. A key aspect of his temperament, that is to say, strengthened by
his own experiences and by his Polish background, mirrored and reinforced the menace implicit in the subject
matter of the adventure mode.

Conrad was aware of the menace. Toward the end of his
career especially, with lucid honesty in some of his author's notes and with triumphant art in *The Shadow-Line*
(1917), he seems completely conscious of the dangers to
which his temperamental biases and his subject matter
wed him. Indeed, *The Shadow-Line* seems to offer a kind
of mature commentary on the attitudes and presumptions
that animate much of Conrad's early fiction. And in 1920,
in the author's note to *Within the Tides* from which I
quoted briefly earlier, Conrad writes explicitly about what
he calls his "romanticism"—and in terms that demonstrate clearly how aware and perhaps even (as Morton
Zabel suggests) [40] how apologetic he had become about it:

> The nature of the knowledge, suggestions or hints used in
> my imaginative work has depended directly on the condi-
> tions of my active life. It depended more on contacts, and
> very slight contacts at that, than on actual experience; be-
> cause my life as a matter of fact was far from being adven-
> turous in itself. Even now when I look back on it with a
> certain regret (who would not regret his youth?) and posi-

tive affection, its colouring wears the sober hue of hard work and exacting calls of duty, things which in themselves are not much charged with a feeling of romance. If these things appeal strongly to me even in retrospect it is, I suppose, because the romantic feeling of reality was in me an inborn faculty. This in itself may be a curse but when disciplined by a sense of personal responsibility and a recognition of the hard facts of existence . . . becomes but a point of view from which the very shadows of life appear endowed with an internal glow. And such romanticism is not a sin. It is none the worse for the knowledge of truth. It only tries to make the best of it. [pp. v–vi]

The discipline of which he speaks in this passage came to him only intermittently, and it is a poignant fact that Conrad's full conscious awareness of the dangers to which he was prey comes at that point in his career when, apparently wearied and faltering, though he can speak of the rigor his art requires, he can no longer summon it. (The dull attempts at irony in *Chance* [1913]—notably in the subtitles to the various sections of the novel: "The Knight," "The Damsel," etc.—hint perhaps at Conrad's recognition of the need for a distancing rigor and of his declining capacities for achieving it.) It is also moving to realize that this late, important statement of artistic conscience prefaces one of Conrad's least impressive volumes, a collection of four stories (written during the period 1911–14 and first published in book form in 1915) not one of which is worthy of the author of *Under Western Eyes*.

The double threat presented by his exotic material and by the natural inclinations of his temperament render Conrad's failures a good deal more interesting than the successes of many other writers. For the realization that "Gaspar Ruiz" (1906) and *Nostromo* have nearly identical

origins in their author's fundamental interests and responses must help us to study—and, especially, to value
—the nature of Conrad's achievement in *Nostromo*. To
examine Conrad from the perspective indicated above,
then, should help us to learn just what Conrad did when
he wrote well, and it should hint at what went wrong
when he wrote badly.

Such a perspective should also begin to explain why
Conrad is perhaps the most uneven great writer in English. At first glance, to be sure, one ought to be puzzled
by the fact that in the *'Twixt Land and Sea* volume
(1912) so fine a story as "The Secret Sharer" is framed by
the embarrassing operatics of "A Smile of Fortune" and
"Freya of the Seven Isles." Or that during the period in
which he was writing *Lord Jim* and *Heart of Darkness*
Conrad was also at work with Ford on *Romance*. But
these anomalies disappear once we recognize that unlike
the technical or emotional problems which most writers
must confront and solve, Conrad's central difficulty was
not one that a single successful book or technical discovery could eliminate. With each novel or story the pressures toward falseness and exaggeration renewed themselves. And what is more, those pressures were never
specific or localized, were never simply a question of getting the plot right or excising a purple passage; they
threatened instead to infect every aspect of his work,
from the smallest details of sentence and paragraph to
the largest strategies of plot and structure and overall tone.
The history of Conrad's career is thus a history of unre-
mitting crisis. Not the simpler, though quite terrible and
real, financial crisis which his letters eloquently chronicle.
Nor the more serious crisis, recounted also in the letters,
of his long days and weeks of imaginative paralysis. The
great crisis, the recurring crisis, was the need for continual
vigilance in the face of personal inclinations which con-

spired with his typical subject matter to cry aloud for simplification, for extravagance, for untruth. Conrad's precarious achievement of that vigilance is a recurring concern in the chapters which follow.

2   Minor Conrad: *Romance* and Other Works

Robert Louis Stevenson died in Samoa in 1894, the year preceding the publication of *Almayer's Folly*. In the same year Anthony Hope (1863–1933) published his enormously successful and not quite forgotten costume romance, *The Prisoner of Zenda;* [1] Hope's fellow romancer Stanley Weyman (1855–1928) came out with *Under the Red Robe,* a historical novel which "neatly reduced the matter of Dumas to the dimensions of circulating-library readers"; [2] and Rudyard Kipling, whose stories of British India had already attracted wide attention, published *The Jungle Book.* The public taste for the exotic and the adventurous, a taste that had asserted itself in the 1880s when Rider Haggard (1856–1925) conquered a huge readership with the African settings and exciting narrative thrust of *King Solomon's Mines* (1885), *She* (1887), and *Allan Quatermain* (1887), was in the ascendant. [3]

Stevenson's enormous prominence in the late-Victorian world of Conrad's apprentice years is strikingly clear in Quiller-Couch's extravagant eulogy:

> Put away books and paper and pen. Stevenson is dead, and now there is nobody left to write for. . . . For five years the needle of literary endeavour in Great Britain has quivered towards a little island in the South Pacific, as to its magnetic pole. [4]

Stevenson's death was the occasion of a similar lament in the pages of the same highly regarded journal that would from the first honor Conrad. And the terms of that lament clarify, perhaps, some of the reasons for Conrad's acceptance by publishers, reviewers, and editors, even as they help to explain his years of unpopularity with the general public:

> The most striking individuality in English letters of to-day has gone from us. He was the laureate of the joy of life, of the life here and now. . . . The world was getting tired of analysis and introspection. . . . He took us out into the open air and made us care for the common life and adventures of men.[5]

Though his contemporaries did not perceive it, the escapist elements in Stevenson's work are far from dominant in his later books, several of which anticipate with distinction Conrad's treatment of similar characters and themes.[6] But escape is obviously central to the Stevenson of *Treasure Island* (1883) and of most of the essays (1876–82) in *The Cornhill Magazine* that first established his popularity. The fable of faraway places, peopled with vigorous heroes and filled with exciting action and exotic mysteries, was a staple of the reading public through the last fifteen years of the nineteenth century and the first decade of the twentieth.

Conrad himself, in his most significant collaboration with Ford Madox Ford, made a conscious contribution to this body of escapist literature. And *Romance* (1903), though far from successful even in its own modest terms, is a remarkably clear example of Conrad's interest in the situations and relationships that are fundamental to adventure fiction at all levels of sophistication. Though the novel gives us Conrad at low voltage, he is still recognizably Conrad.

He had few illusions about the book and seems to have regarded it primarily as a money-making project.[7] Within a month of the novel's publication, he wrote to a Polish friend in a vein of slightly embarrassed apology:

There are certain things that are difficult to explain, especially after they have happened. I consider *Romance* as
something of no importance; I collaborated on it at a
time when it was impossible for me to do anything else. It
was easy to relate a few events without being otherwise involved in the subject. The idea we had was purely aesthetic: to depict in an appropriate way certain scenes and
certain situations. Also it did not displease us to be able
to show that we could do something which was very
much en vogue with the public at the moment. The heroic gospel of St. Henry, dear Sir, rules the entire world
and, as you know, there is more than one way of laughing
at it. There were moments when both Hueffer and I were
very gay while working on this construction. Nevertheless
we took pains with the technical side of the work. You
will admit that it is well written. Flaubert (he was a real
saint) applied himself well to achieve a spectacular success.[8]

And to Galsworthy, referring to the novel by its original
title, he wrote: *"Seraphina* is finished and gone out of the
house she has haunted for this year past. I do really hope
it will hit the taste of the street—unless the devil's in it." [9]

Ford, too, in his engaging account of the collaboration
suggests that Conrad's initial interest in the manuscript
which became *Romance* was largely material. In an amus-
ing passage from his first memoir of Conrad, Ford describes Conrad's disappointment with his friend's first
draft: he had expected, but not found, something as "far
flung in popularity as *Treasure Island* but as 'written' as
Salammbo, by the addition to which of a few touches of
description, sea-atmosphere, and the like, in a fortnight
. . . fortune should lie at the feet of the adventurers." [10]
Financial motives aside, the idea of collaboration must
have appealed particularly to Conrad as a means of com-
bating his dispiriting periods of artistic barrenness and his
constitutional inability to write quickly. Indeed, he had

suggested collaboration to his friend Edward Noble three years prior to his arrangement with Ford.[11]

We should be wronging Conrad, however, if we assumed that his commitment to *Romance*—a commitment that extended over at least four years—was entirely devoid of artistic purpose. Even his own explanation of the book as a technical challenge cannot tell the whole story. Although he never felt the collaboration to be as important as his own writing, it seems clear that his intentions were less mercenary and more respectable than some scholars have suggested.[12] In a fit of characteristic gloom in the late spring of 1902, just a few months before *Romance* was finally completed, Conrad wrote to Garnett:

> The Blackwood vol: shall be coming out in two three months: *Youth Heart of Dark* [88] and a thing I am trying to write now called the *End of the Tether*—an inept title to heartbreaking bosh. Pawling's vol. shall follow at a decent interval; four stories of which Typhoon is first and best. I am ashamed of them all; I don't believe either in their popularity or in their merit. Strangely enough it is yet my share of *Romance* (collab[on] stuff with Ford) that fills me with the least dismay.[13]

Even at the outset of the collaboration, Conrad's interest in the "novel about Cuban pirates" that Ford had described to him was in part an interest in the serious possibilities of the subject.[14] As he wrote to W. E. Henley, in whose *New Review The Nigger of the "Narcissus"* had been serialized a year earlier:

> When talking with Hueffer my first thought was that the man there who couldn't find a publisher had some good stuff to use and that if we worked it up together my name, probably, would get a publisher for it. On the other hand I thought that working with him would keep under the particular devil that spoils my work for me as quick as I turn it out (that's why I work so slow and

> break my word to publishers), and that *the material
> being of the kind that appeals to my imagination* and the
> man being an honest workman we could turn out some-
> thing tolerable—perhaps.[15]

This seems to me a fair summary of Conrad's motives in
suggesting the collaboration. His own slowness was a factor, of course; so was his hope for financial reward. But it
is a mistake to discount the imaginative appeal Ford's
work-in-progress must have held for the man who described his earliest intentions for *The Rescue* as follows:
"I want to make it a kind of glorified book for boys—you
know. No analysis. No damned mouthing. Pictures—
pictures—pictures. That's what I want to do." [16] Or for
the writer whose most eloquent defense of his work included, centrally, this passage:

> The favourable critics of ["Youth"] . . . remarked with a
> sort of surprise "This after all is a story for boys yet—"
>   Exactly. Out of the material of a boys' story I've made
> *Youth* by the force of the idea expressed in accordance
> with a strict conception of my method. And however un-
> favourably it may affect the business in hand I must
> confess that I shall not depart from my method.[17]

If we compare these statements with Conrad's remarkably
similar comments about *Romance*—

> The book . . . is NOT a boy's story . . . the aim being to
> present the scenes and events and people *strictly realisti-
> cally* in a glamour of *Romance* . . . a serious attempt at
> *interesting, animated Romance* with no more psychology
> than comes naturally into the action.[18]—

it becomes difficult to deny the genuine seriousness of his
commitment to the novel.[19]

   That Conrad was far from reluctant to accept a large
part of the responsibility for *Romance* is clear from his inscription in Curle's copy:

In this book I have done my share of writing. Most of the characters (with the exception of Mrs. Williams, Seabright and the seamen) were introduced by Hueffer and developed then in my own way with, of course, his consent and collaboration. The last part is (like the first) the work of Hueffer, except a few pars. written by me. Part second is actually joint work. Parts 3 & 4 are my writing, with here and there a sentence by Hueffer.[20]

Since the divisions in the book are not of equal length, by this reckoning—elsewhere he claimed a somewhat smaller share for himself[21]—Conrad wrote considerably more than 300 of the novel's 541 pages unaided and shared in the writing of another 82. Moreover, his dependence on Ford's initial conception is not in itself especially significant. He freely acknowledged several times that his "inventive faculty . . . was never very strong,"[22] and there is a sense in which *Romance* would fit much less easily into the corpus of Conrad's work if he had himself invented the essentials of the story. The circumstances which led to the collaboration—Conrad hearing from Ford the story of a young man's trial for piracy and finding the anecdote imaginatively stimulating—are perfectly congruent with Conrad's usual beginnings. I do not believe Ford exaggerated Conrad's interest in the anecdote about pirates that was the germ of the novel, and his witty account of Conrad's annoyance with the first draft of the book strikes me as shrewd and wholly authentic. Listening with manifest displeasure to Ford's reading, Conrad remained "shut up in the depth of his disappointment and still more in his reprobation of the criminal who could take hold of such a theme and not, gripping it by the throat, extract from it every drop of blood and glamour."[23]

In other respects, too, the genesis of *Romance* is typical of Conrad. This is particularly true of the story's founda-

tions in historically verifiable fact. Conrad frequently re-
searched his books, often in libraries and museums,[24] and
the letter to Blackwood in which he outlines the plot of
Romance resembles nothing so much as one of those author's notes in which Conrad describes in detail—as if
anxious to persuade us that there really *was* a Mr. Jones,
that someone's faithful retainer really *had* stolen a lighter-
full of silver—the personal or historical origins of the
book he has written:

> This tale—which we call a romance—has been grubbed
> out of the British Museum by Hueffer. All the details of
> the political feeling in Jamaica (about 1821) are authen-
> tic. There was really a perfectly innocent young English-
> man who was tried for piracy and escaped the gallows by
> the merest hair's-breadth. There did exist a nest of pirates
> about that time on the coast of Cuba. They were a sorry
> lot—I admit. O'Brien [the chief villain] is our own inven-
> tion, and he is possible enough—I mean historically pos-
> sible. Good many Irishmen took refuge in Spain, made
> careers, and founded families.[25]

And in the pattern of its mutation from historical fact
into completed novel, *Romance* is entirely representative
of Conrad's work. Like *Lord Jim,* the book vastly elaborates the real incident on which it was based. Indeed, in
its evolution from Ford's anecdote through its various
stages and synopses, *Romance* illustrates almost as clearly
as *Nostromo* what John Halverson and Ian Watt have
called "two of the most characteristic features of Conrad's
imagination: parsimony of invention, prodigality of
discovery." [26] As with most of Conrad's fiction, the novel's
plot is more the result of decisions taken in the act of
writing than of some predetermined plan, and the book
itself differs radically from the interim summary of the
story that Conrad and Ford drew up early in their collaboration.[27]

In every case, these discrepancies call attention to strengths in the finished book. In the synopsis Kemp's adventures are only loosely tied together, the dangers he encounters often coming into the story arbitrarily and not in consequence of what has gone before. The summary of the book thus violates one of Conrad and Ford's central principles: "Before everything, a story must convey a sense of inevitability: that which happens in it must seem to be the only thing that could have happened." [28] But if we will allow Kemp the right to fall in love during the course of his story—and, surely, any hero of romantic adventure is entitled to that—then it is fair to say that for the most part the novel, whatever its other failings, respects the principle of inevitability. Consider, for example, the beginning of the synopsis:

> The story begins in a farmhouse in Kent, goes on in Jamaica, then on the Cuban Coast and ends in England.
> The narrator John Kemp, driven out of his home by his mother's severity, walks down to Hythe: falls in with some smugglers; joins them recklessly in a "tub-raising" expedition during which the boat sinks; and is rescued by an outward bound ship.[29]

The opening of the novel is much tighter than this and carefully establishes a more credible background for Kemp's departure from England and for his subsequent entanglements with the law, with the pirates, and with the Riego family. In the synopsis Kemp's involvement with the smugglers is the result of a whim (he "falls in" with them and "recklessly" joins their current adventure), his rescue by "an outward bound ship" which takes him to Jamaica and to pirate country is fortuitous, and there is no mention of the Riegos, the Spanish family living in Cuba to whose fortunes he becomes committed. In the novel these weaknesses are eliminated. Carlos Riego and his

faithful retainer Thomas Castro, both of whom play a central role in Kemp's adventures, are introduced in the very
first pages, and since Riego is the cousin of Kemp's future
brother-in-law, his presence in the novel and his connection with Kemp are, even from the start, not accidental.
Partly because of his desire for adventure and partly because he wants to help his brother-in-law avoid the risk of
personal scandal on the eve of his wedding, Kemp agrees
to help Riego and Castro (who is wanted for piracy) escape from the authorities by making contact with the (historically valid) smugglers who infest the Kentish coast.
Mistaken by officers of the Crown for a smuggler and
nearly captured, Kemp is forced to flee from England with
the romantic semi-bandits he had sought to help. In the
prologue to his adventures, then, Kemp's relationship
with the Riego family is firmly established, and this, together with his status as a fugitive and not a mere adventurer, gives to the complications that follow a force and
credibility not possible in the less rigorously plotted synopsis.

The whole novel is as carefully designed, and differs in
nearly the same degree from the synopsis, as these opening
pages. Within the Stevensonian conventions by which
they must be judged, the events of *Romance* comprise a
progressive sequence of intensifying danger and excitement into which each new development fits logically and
even inevitably.[30]

That Stevenson should be the measure of this novel is,
of course, perfectly just. Conrad himself admitted as much
when he warned Ford in a letter that if he indicated publicly that *Romance* had taken six years to write, the critics
would compare its joint authors unfavorably with "R.L.S.
[who], singlehanded, produce[s] his masterpieces."[31] It
is even possible, as Thomas Moser has suggested to me,
that Stevenson's example influenced Conrad in his deci-

sion to request the collaboration. In financial need and
imaginatively played out,[32] Conrad may well have recalled
that Stevenson—and, for that matter, Kipling—had collaborated on novels that had been widely popular. In a
letter to Conrad concerning his plan to work jointly with
Ford, W. E. Henley mentioned the Stevenson–Lloyd Osbourne collaborations. Conrad claimed in his reply to
have been surprised by Henley's references to Stevenson
and to Dumas: "These are big names and I assure you it
had never occurred to me they could be pronounced in
connection with my plan to work with Hueffer. But you
have judged proper to pronounce them and I am bound
to look seriously at that aspect of the matter." [33] Whether
such comparisons had occurred to him earlier, or whether
Henley's remarks called his attention to them, is less important than the fact that in working on *Romance* Conrad
had the author of *Treasure Island* firmly in mind.

There are, in either case, some notable resemblances between *Romance* and Stevenson's tightly plotted adventure
tales, and *Kidnapped* (1886) as well as its sequel *Catriona*
(1893) have an especially direct bearing on the
Conrad–Ford novel.[34] Although it is fairly clear that Conrad did not think highly of Stevenson,[35] and although we
can scarcely claim that the collaborators composed *Romance* with an open copy of *Treasure Island* near to
hand,[36] there can be no doubt of the Stevenson influence.
The Conrad letters which refer to Stevenson are evidence
enough. And we must remember, also, that it is quite as difficult to conceive of a writer in English at the turn of the
century beginning an avowed adventure tale without a
keen awareness of Stevenson's example as it is to imagine
a contemporary American novelist of the South who is
free of Faulkner's influence.

Like both *Kidnapped* and *Catriona, Romance* is set in
a past that is not too distant—the real-life prototype of

John Kemp was tried at the Old Bailey in 1824—and in a fairly realistic locale. That we are never fully convinced of the reality of the setting, just as we are never entirely convinced in Stevenson's non-Scottish adventure fiction, is a measure of Conrad's relative distance from his materials, the clear limits of his engagement in the story. But what must be emphasized is that however unconvincing the setting of *Romance* is, its unreality is different in kind from that of a novel like *The Prisoner of Zenda,* where the reader knows that the locale is an elegant construct, a fairy-tale land whose fanciful artificiality is, indeed, part of its charm, but in whose shimmering air no real person ever drew breath.

Apart from their similar attitude toward setting, the two Stevenson novels resemble *Romance* in several more specific ways. Stevenson's hero in both books is David Balfour, a callow but strong-hearted, conventionally reared young fellow with an acute sense of honor who seems in many ways the ancestor of the similarly presented hero of *Romance.* What is more, the very events of *Romance* may owe something to *Catriona,* for both books—though *Romance* far more centrally—focus on the adventures of a young man fleeing his enemies across strange country in the company of the girl he loves and must protect. Finally, in all three books this young hero is also the narrator of his story, and in all three his telling ostensibly occurs many years after the events. But neither Stevenson nor Conrad and Ford turn this potentially rich perspective to any serious use. Conrad and Ford try rather clumsily to do so, however, and in thus parting company with Stevenson's unpretentious adventure tales they damage their book beyond repair. This damage, moreover, is of particular interest for students of Conrad, since the nature of his failure with *Romance* prefigures the weaknesses of a good deal of the fiction of his last years.

In *Kidnapped,* as in all of his adventure stories, Steven-

son wisely allows his great gift for narrative to dominate.
Even in *The Master of Ballantrae* (1889), his most distinguished finished achievement in pure adventure, a book
with a formal complexity of which Stevenson was fully
conscious—in the dedication he speaks of "the problem
of Mackellar's homespun [narration] and how to shape it
for superior flights" [37]—even there Stevenson's sense of
pace and his inventiveness in devising exciting actions are
given full play. Now *Romance,* especially in its third and
fourth sections (written, incidentally, primarily by Conrad), does have a vigorous and appropriately suspenseful
plot. Conrad was responsible for the vigor, and it is a mistake to take his various remarks about the "mere material" of his fiction to mean that he actually despised physical action.[38] Discussing their ways of working, Ford makes
an incisive comment about Conrad's temperament which
tells us much not only about the Conrad who collaborated
on two rather slight novels and one worthless fragment
but also about the artist who wrote *Lord Jim* and *Under
Western Eyes:*

> The differences in our temperaments were sufficiently
> well marked. Conrad was brave: he was for inclusion and
> hang the consequences. The writer [Ford], more circum-
> spect, was for ever on the watch to suppress the melodra-
> matic incident and the sounding phrase. . . . "You must
> invent [Conrad said]. You have got to make that fellow
> live perpetually under the shadow of the gallows." [39]

Though if unchecked these impulses, as I suggested in my
first chapter, constitute one of the greatest dangers to Conrad's fiction, their value for a writer of adventure stories is
quite clear. That they found expression in *Romance* is the
book's strength:

> I've studied p. III as a whole very earnestly. It is most
> important and it wants doing over. It must be given hard
> *reality.* The treatment as it stands is too much in the air

—in places. I don't want to bother you now by going
into the argument. I shall do the thing myself, but of
course I would want to speak to you about it.[40]

Frank MacShane, in an illuminating discussion of Conrad's contributions to *Romance,* rightly emphasizes the extent to which Conrad simplified the narrative line of the
novel and clarified its personal relationships. Though one
wonders whether the book's earlier subtlety was genuine,
it is difficult to dissent from MacShane's conclusion:
"What is lost [in consequence of Conrad's revisions],
then, is a certain subtlety, but the lucidity and suspense
that is gained is certainly more important in this sort of
novel." [41]

The trouble is that neither Conrad nor Ford—it would
be unfair and certainly inaccurate to blame Ford alone—
could refrain from "explaining" the story in a commentary of deadly grandiloquence. The novel is choked with
sentences and whole paragraphs in which Kemp tries to
extract from his adventures some general moral significa-
tion. The contemporary reviewer who thought it was "a
pity to let a good, sound hero, in the midst of all his dangers" stop to discuss Life and Romance erred only by
being too good-natured about his complaint.[42] The following passages are typical:

> How often the activity of our life is the least real part
> of it! Life, looked upon as a whole, presents itself to my
> fancy as a pursuit with open arms of a winged and mag-
> nificent dream, hovering just over our heads and casting
> its glory upon our hopes. It is in this simple vision, which
> is one and enduring, and not in the changing facts, that
> we must look for meaning and for truth. [p. 335]

> I had fought a harder battle with a more cruel foe than
> death, with the doubt of myself; an endless contest, in
> which there is no peace of victory or of defeat. The open

sea was like a blank and unscalable wall imprisoning the eternal question of conduct. Right or wrong? Generosity or folly? Conscience or only weak fear before remorse? The magnificent ritual of sunset went on palpitating with an inaudible rhythm, with slow and unerring observance, went on to the end, leaving its funeral fires on the sky and a great shadow upon the sea. [p. 331]

And, looking back, we see Romance—that subtle thing that is mirage—that is life. . . . Looking back, it seems a wonderful enough thing that I who am this, and she who is that, commencing so far away a life that, after such sufferings borne together and apart, ended so tranquilly in a world so stable—that she and I should have passed through so much, good chance and evil chance, sad hours and joyful, all lived down and swept away into the little heap of dust that is life. That, too, is Romance! [p. 541] [43]

That the oppressive, grandiloquent explicitness of these paragraphs, and especially of the first two, poisons with banality themes that are essential to Conrad's mature achievement simply indicates how potentially Conradian are the materials of *Romance* and underscores the truth of this observation from the "Familiar Preface" to *A Personal Record:* "In this matter of life and art it is not the Why that matters so much to our happiness as the How. As the Frenchman said, *'Il y a toujours la manière.'* Very true. Yes. There is the manner" (p. xix).

The unredeemed pretentiousness which undermines *Romance* prefigures the very note of the later Conrad, and the subtitle of part five—"The Lot of Man"—captures exactly the tone of disappointing novels like *Chance* (1913) or *The Rescue* (1920). Conrad had a weakness for such grandiose subtitles, but usually—as in *Nostromo*—was able to control it. In their portent-laden pseudo-glamor, the subtitles of *The Rescue* offend exactly as *Romance* offends: "The Man and the Brig," "The Gift of the Shallows"; or, worse yet, "The Point of Honour and the Point of Passion," "The Claim of Life and the Toll of Death"! Such excesses, we must however reluctantly admit, came all too easily to Conrad. And if they seem to have come rather more insistently in his last years, they were scarcely, as *Romance* shows, a new development but were instead the expression of a weakness to which he had been prone from the very first.

In another way, too, *Romance* casts ahead to those bad books Conrad wrote in his last years. For in *Romance,* though in somewhat restrained shape, the figure of the impotent hero makes an appearance.[44] John Kemp shares with Monsieur George of *The Arrow of Gold* (1919), with several other characters from Conrad's later novels, and (in a final parallel with Stevenson's *Kidnapped* and *Catriona*) with David Balfour a curious incapacity for action at crucial moments in his story. Kemp several times finds himself unable to kill O'Brien, his archenemy, and also loses through indecision the opportunity to kill the pirate leader Manuel del Popolo, who is a secondary villain in the novel. These moments are explained in *Romance* by the claim that Kemp's conscience won't allow him to kill men who are defenseless: it is a version of the British public school morality which, to do the novel justice, is mocked repeatedly by Kemp's partner, the Spaniard Thomas Castro. But such an explanation nonetheless sharply distinguishes *Romance* from Conrad's serious adventure fiction, where the hero's hestitant unreadiness is a fact of his humanity and not, as here, allegedly a commitment to principle. Moreover, this easy solution to Kemp's indecisiveness becomes, perhaps, less than satisfying when we see Kemp *in extremis*, hidden in a cave with his beloved, passively hoping the pirates outside will go away without bothering him. It is a scene that recalls the very similar moment in *The Arrow of Gold* when Monsieur George, playing Kemp to Rita's Seraphina, trembles silently behind a locked door while the villain Ortega rages in impotent fury outside.

But to recognize that the weaknesses of *Romance* are typically Conradian is scarcely to exhaust the book's relevance to Conrad's oeuvre. I have already suggested, for example, that its grounding in historical fact and its sharp divergence from the synopsis Conrad and Ford had composed argue its affinities with most of Conrad's major work. And what is more important still is the simple fact that the essential materials of *Romance* are also those of, say, *Lord Jim* and *Nostromo*.

The relationship between *Romance* and *Nostromo* is particularly close. In fact, Ford actually wrote at least sixteen manuscript pages of the latter when Conrad was too ill to work, and Conrad planned to depend on Ford for additional help if it became necessary.[45] *Romance* was still in progress when Conrad began *Nostromo,* and as Frederick Karl rightly observes, the collaboration "provided a trial ground" for the later book.[46]

In both novels a crucial, perhaps *the* crucial scene involves an escape by night from a harbor that is infested with enemies; in both books the escape is made in a small boat, and in both the fugitive-heroes, protected by fog, narrowly evade capture. There seems little doubt that Kemp's flight in Rio Medio Bay in company with his pirate retainer Thomas Castro is an early version of Decoud and Nostromo's venture into Sulaco harbor with the treasure of silver. Moreover, as Karl notes, Conrad's handling of the mob scenes in *Nostromo* is obviously indebted to his similar descriptions of the rabble Lugareños who make life so difficult for John Kemp in *Romance*.[47]

And there are other important resemblances between

the two novels: *Romance* is in some measure interested in locating the springs of human action in illusion and obsession (only abstractly, of course: the theme is not dramatized); and the book, too, though in halting and indecisive fashion, deals with the problems of an undeveloped Latin American country whose political instability permits disreputable bandits of various sorts to exploit the population for their own unpretty ends. Indeed, one of the most interesting characters in the novel is the villain O'Brien, whose obsessive hatred of the English and equally obsessive love of Seraphina feeds his genius for demagogy and frenzied political scheming. He is treated at important moments with excessive melodrama—as, for example, in his interview late in the book with Kemp, who refuses to tell him whether Seraphina is still alive:

> Then I saw that he was crying.
> "The curse—the curse of Cromwell on you," he sobbed suddenly. "You send me back to hell again." He writhed his whole body. "Sorrow!" he said, "I know it. But what's this? What's *this?*" [p. 469]

And, a few harangues later:

> "You cold, pitiless, English scoundrel," he shrieked suddenly. The breaking down of his restraint had let him go right into madness. "You have murdered her." [p. 473]

But O'Brien remains nonetheless a sharply drawn character who at times reminds one of Conrad's other men of obsession—of the melodramatic villains of the later books, to be sure, but also of the ill-favored old captain in "Youth" and of the credible and memorable figure of Almayer, on his knees near the end of Conrad's first novel, "creeping along the sand, eras[ing] carefully with his hand all traces of Nina's footsteps" (p. 195).

These specific parallels aside, *Romance* remains an essentially Conradian fiction whose narrative mode, whose plot and setting, whose central characters reappear, transformed and chastened but still recognizable, in Conrad's finest work. That the novel is disappointing, that it fails to exploit meaningfully its full energies, does not in the least imply that its substance is alien to Conrad.[48] Further, as I suggested in chapter 1, the very fact of the book's failure is useful to us: first, because that failure reminds us of the rigor and vigilance and conscious intelligence that Conrad must have expended in the writing of his great fiction; and second, because it shows us the extent to which Conrad's major achievement is founded, often, on the recurring, even *defining*, features of the traditional adventure story. Robert Kiely's catalogue of the basic ingredients of "the adventure story in its conventional, almost sub-literary, sense" describes *Romance* almost as well as the early Stevenson: "a concatenation of faraway places, bizarre characters, sea voyages, mysterious benefactors, abductions, duels, endless flights from hostile pursuers, and seemingly endless quests for unattainable goals." [49]

Most of these elements—we must, I suppose, exclude the mysterious benefactors—are clearly enough the materials not just of *Romance,* but of Conrad's other texts as well. Their exotic settings require no comment. But it is perhaps worth recalling that pursuit and flight are fundamental Conradian motifs; that abductions move the plots in stories and novels written at every stage of Conrad's career; that the bizarre character whom Kiely names as a staple of adventure fiction is a recurring figure in the weak as well as the strong Conrad; and finally, that duels, hand-to-hand combat, natural catastrophe, extreme physical suffering, violent death—all the blood and thunder of the traditional narrative of outdoor adventure—are the

very substance of Conrad's world. That the *Tremolino* episode in *The Mirror of the Sea* (1906), purporting to be
autobiography, relies directly on the conventions of the
adventure yarn is striking evidence for the centrality of
such conventions in Conrad's way of seeing the world and
in his way of writing about it.

  Romance, then, differs from Conrad's greater works not
because its substance is untypical of him but because that
substance, for the most part, remains lifeless, conventional, uninteresting. In this novel—as in most of his unsuccessful fiction and particularly in what Marvin Mudrick has justly called the "fag-end adventure-stuff" of his
last years [50]—Conrad does not extract from the commonplace themes and circumstances of the adventure story the
latent energies he discovers in *Lord Jim, Nostromo, The
Shadow-Line, Heart of Darkness,* "The Secret Sharer."

  Conrad and Ford's unconvincing treatment of John
Kemp illustrates this failure most clearly even as it reminds us of the fact that the type of the young hero,
dragged unready into a world of moral and physical menace, is both a cliché of the adventure mode and a figure of
seminal importance in Conrad's finest books. Kemp is a
particularly lifeless hero, whose inability to act decisively
during moments of crisis I have already commented on.
Though the novel makes a half-hearted effort to suggest
that the physical trials its hero undergoes mature and
change him, the narrating voice of the older Kemp, looking back on his days of youth and high adventure, is the
least effective aspect of the novel. This is especially true of
those passages in which the speaker discusses the moral dimensions of his experiences:

> I was maturing in the fire of love, of danger; in the lurid
> light of life piercing through my youthful innocence. [p.
> 203]

I was young, and my belief in the justice of life had received a shock. If it were impossible to foretell the consequences of our acts, if there was no safety in the motives within ourselves, what remained for our guidance? [p. 429]

The second passage raises, abstractly, important issues: the very dilemmas of Decoud, of Jim, of the narrator-heroes in *The Shadow-Line* and "The Secret Sharer." In *Romance,* however, even when such musings are not (as in the first passage above) instantly exposed by their own magniloquence, they remain mere assertions; they are not shown to be dramatically true; they affect neither plot nor character. And so the serious implications of such passages are never exploited in *Romance.* The conventional adventure narrative—*Romance,* Stevenson's *Treasure Island* or *Kidnapped,* Marryat's *Mr. Midshipman Easy* (1836) are all, in this respect, models of the kind—very often comprises a simplified variation on the *bildungsroman,* with the youthful protagonist undergoing his education in an exotic and unfamiliar locale. In his serious novels, too, Conrad frequently relies upon such a hero, but he exploits the full potentials of the convention; he focuses equally upon the physical ordeals his characters must face and upon the interior crises those ordeals create. What is latent in Kemp's forced assertions about his loss of innocence and his self-doubt becomes the full, controlled subject of the *Tremolino* episode (where Conrad sticks as close as possible to the adventure model without surrendering to its simplicities), of the great first-person sea stories, of *Lord Jim,* and of *Heart of Darkness.* The adventure ingredients are essential to these books, but they are more fully and more responsibly used.

The same may be said of the way in which *Romance* adumbrates what I have come to believe is a crucial relationship both for Conrad and for the typical adventure tale: a relationship between the young hero, inexperienced and facing tests of his physical and moral courage; and another man, usually older, whose appearance (he is often maimed or scarred in an ominous, romantic way) and commitments are vaguely unlawful and whose familiarity with the alien world in which his young accomplice moves is intimate and often professional. This older man acts usually as a guide and teacher and protector of the younger one, though he may also implicitly (and explicitly in some of Conrad's best fiction) menace the young man. In its most conventional version, the relation between these two figures involves a bond of loyalty that is almost feudal, in which the older man, for all his greater competence and experience, acts the part of faithful retainer to the young man's hero. But in this role the older character retains a large measure of authority, for he is the initiate, intimate with the rituals and perils his young friend must learn, with his help, to master or to endure. Nearly always this partner is a man of great physical courage who has survived a history of struggle with exotic nature, has lived the life of an outlaw, or has fought in many wars. Often he is an Indian or a native, his very blood thus linking him to the exotic and the primitive.

A relation between such a figure and the hero would appear to be central to any literature concerned with the theme of initiation and concerned to celebrate or scrutinize the masculine virtues of courage and physical prowess, for it is found in stories and folk myths at all levels of seriousness: from Prince Hal and Falstaff to the Lone Ranger and Tonto; from Don Quixote and Sancho Panza to David Balfour and Alan Breck in *Kidnapped;* from Ishmael and Queequeg to John Kemp and Thomas Castro in *Romance.*

Castro, indeed, is the most interesting and convincing

character in *Romance,* and from one angle its true hero. Like any traditional retainer-type, Castro is a man of action, contemptuous of moral delicacy, pragmatic and expert in the art of survival. Whereas Kemp's escapes from danger remain throughout the novel almost wholly fortuitous, Castro makes his own luck. As Kemp himself remarks late in the novel: "It was obvious to me that, had it not been for [Castro], we two, lost and wandering in the storm, should have died from exposure and exhaustion— from some accident perhaps" (p. 363). Repeatedly, Castro rescues Kemp and his sweetheart, and in the end he is forced to save them by the sacrifice of his own life. Conrad uses the device of the faithful retainer whose loyalty extends even to the point of dying for his master not only in this novel but in other disappointing works like "Gaspar Ruiz" and *The Rover* (1923), where the faithful retainer becomes the protagonist.

Castro's death, however, is not presented to us with entirely stereotyped simplicity. Twice he nearly betrays his friends to the bandits who have captured him, and in the climactic moment, on the precipice near the mouth of the cave in which Kemp and Seraphina are concealed, Castro stammers in terror, then recovers himself, tells the saving lie that Kemp and the girl have drowned and throws himself over the cliff. About his motives, as (more seriously) about Lord Jim's, we are left uncertain:

> He had his own courage after all—if only the courage not to believe in Manuel's promises. And he must have been weary of his life—weary enough not to pay that price. And yet he had gone to the very verge, calling upon Seraphina as if she could hear him. Madness of fear, no doubt—succeeded by an awakening, a heroic reaction. And yet sometimes it seems to me as if the whole scene, with his wild cries for help, had been the outcome of a supreme exercise of cunning. [pp. 402–03]

Castro's vacillations and falterings humanize him; and
there are, too, hints of complexity in his fits of pique over
Kemp's refusal to kill unarmed enemies and also in his
surprising openness in moments of repose: "The warmth
of the fire had penetrated our chilled bodies with a feeling of comfort. . . . Williams' flask was empty; and this
was a new Castro, mellowed, discursive, almost genial"
(p. 363). Castro is not at every moment the tightlipped
warrior: he comes as near as anyone in this novel to being
a flesh-and-blood man. But he remains in all essential
ways the very embodiment of the type of the loyal retainer, and his background is a model of the kind:

> Such as he was—a born vagabond, *contrabandista,* spy in
> armed camps, sutler at the tail of the *Grande Armée* (es-
> caped, God only knows how, from the snows of Russia),
> beggar, *guerillero,* bandit sceptically murderous, draping
> his rags in saturnine dignity—he had ended by becoming
> the sinister and grotesque squire of our quixotic Carlos.
> [p. 253]

These, in substance, are the credentials of Dominic
Cervoni—a "modern and unlawful wanderer with his
own legend of loves, dangers and bloodshed" (*Mirror,* p.
163)—the Corsican sailor of Conrad's youth who appears
twice under his own name in Conrad's writings: in the
Tremolino chapters from *The Mirror of the Sea* and in
The Arrow of Gold, the disappointing late novel that
Conrad claimed was strictly autobiographical. The respect
and affection with which Dominic is treated in both
pieces, and especially in the *Tremolino* episode, are surely
an accurate index of Conrad's attitude toward him and,
more significantly, toward the commitments and life style
he represents. In the character of Nostromo, of course, directly inspired by Dominic, Conrad subjects the type, and
his affections for such men, to the fullest scrutiny:

> Mainly Nostromo is what he is because I received the inspiration for him in my early days from a Mediterranean sailor. Those who have read certain pages of mine will see at once what I mean when I say that Dominic, the padrone of the *Tremolino,* might under given circumstances have been a Nostromo. [*Nostromo,* p. xx]

But the full irony of Nostromo's betrayal, and so the full irony of the novel's encompassing skepticism, depends essentially upon Nostromo's public identity as the loyal retainer to the whole country, "a man absolutely above reproach" (p. 13), "tried and trusty," "the indispensable man" (p. 130).

In both *The Mirror of the Sea* and *The Arrow of Gold* Dominic's taciturn competence is emphasized. He is, so Monsieur George informs us, "the embodiment of fidelity, resource, and courage" (*Arrow,* p. 106). Dominic even impresses the (allegedly) worldly heroine of the novel:

> More than once she said to me: "One would like to put the care of one's personal safety into the hands of that man. He looks as if he simply couldn't fail one." I admitted that this was very true, especially at sea. Dominic couldn't fail. [pp. 106–07]

Like the other potential subjects in this diffuse novel, Dominic's fidelity is never probed or tested. But it is examined, and with some conviction, in the *Tremolino* episode from *The Mirror of the Sea.* Two things about Dominic are especially emphasized in that account: his "piratical," lawless bearing, and his function as a teacher. Conrad is explicit about his younger self's relationship to Dominic:

> "I tell you she is in chase," he affirmed, moodily, after one short glance astern.
> I never doubted his opinion. But with all the ardour of

a neophyte and the pride of an apt learner I was at that
time a great nautical casuist.

"What I can't understand," I insisted, subtly, "is how
on earth, with this wind, she has managed to be just
where she was when we first made her out." [p. 173]

Dominic is to teach his naive friend more than the mere
craft of sailing. Later his "initiated voice" (p. 176) will
compel Conrad to admit the existence of betrayal and
menace and will teach the cost of surviving them.

Though the Dominic of *The Mirror of the Sea,* and to
a still greater extent Thomas Castro, fit with exactness the
part of the faithful retainer, both are serious characters
because Conrad has not allowed the conventional aspects
of the type entirely to obliterate their human qualities.
This is not the case with the Dominic who appears in
The Arrow of Gold, primarily because his function as
teacher or guide is not, in the novel, a significant issue.
The more closely the retainer figure resembles a loyal warrior pure and simple, the less likely he is to engage the serious attention of either the author or his audience.

There are in Conrad's writing both early and late a
number of examples of the retainer figure as virtually
pure stereotype. They are worth noticing briefly because
they remind us of Conrad's recurring dependence on the
type and because they provide a negative standard by
which we can judge, and appreciate more fully, Conrad's
striking treatment of the same sort of figure in his best
work. Among the purely conventional retainers is the old
sword-bearer who guards Karain:

Karain never moved without that attendant, who stood or
squatted close at his back. . . . We noticed that, even
during the most important interviews, Karain would
often give a start, and interrupting his discourse, would
sweep his arm back with a sudden movement, to feel

> whether the old fellow was there. The old fellow, impene-
> trable and weary, was always there. He shared his food,
> his repose, and his thoughts; he knew his plans, guarded
> his secrets; and, impassive behind his master's agitation,
> without stirring the least bit, murmured above his head in
> a soothing tone some words difficult to catch. [*Tales of
> Unrest* (1898), pp. 11, 12]

Karain himself, like Arsat, the narrator in "The Lagoon,"
is cut from the same commonplace cloth. In both these
early stories Conrad is at one with the conventional writers of exotic adventure stories, and the clearest evidence of
this is his use of the exotic setting for mere novelty and
his reliance on the shallowest clichés of the adventure
partnership. Both Karain and Arsat are victims of a fero-
cious remorse, the consequence of their betrayal in the
distant past of their accomplices in adventure. In Arsat's
case the betrayal is the more meaningful because his partner was also his brother. Implicitly, of course, the bond
between allies in adventure is always either fraternal (if
the pair are roughly the same age) or filial (if the retainer
figure is older), but it is, potentially, a daring and enrich-
ing stroke to underscore the relationship by making the
pair literal brothers. Robert Louis Stevenson brilliantly
exploits just such a strategy in *The Master of Ballantrae*.
But Conrad's decision to make Arsat's partner his brother
leads to nothing. Brother or friend, Arsat's companion in
adventure is the simple man of action with no distinguishing physical or psychological characteristics. Even as the
conventional warrior, he lacks distinction: he is Dominic
Cervoni deprived of his mythic dimensions and of his role
as teacher; he is Thomas Castro deprived of his weakness:

> There was no better paddler, no better steersman than
> my brother. Many times, together, we had run races in that
> canoe. . . . There was no braver or stronger man in our
> country than my brother. . . . He knew not fear and no

fatigue . . . My brother! [*Tales of Unrest,* p. 199; last
ellipsis Conrad's]

The pretentious, superliterary phrasing of the next-to-last
sentence and the breathless exclamation at the end of the
passage both indicate that Conrad is here trying to assert
what he cannot show, is trying to *will* into seriousness and
profundity a relationship so stereotyped and shallow that
it will not be quickened into life.

In the disappointing novels of his last years Conrad returns to the stereotype. We can see this clearly in the re-
duction of Dominic Cervoni from the powerfully imagined, almost mythic sailor-teacher of the *Tremolino*
episode to the stock figure he becomes in *The Arrow of
Gold.* It seems, indeed, that one index of Conrad's failing
energies toward the end of his career is the reappearance
in his fiction of the retainer figure who conforms in every
respect to the popular stereotype. The protagonist of *The
Rover* is another example. Old Peyrol is the clear lineal
descendant of Dominic Cervoni and Thomas Castro; his
whole story, in fact, so closely parallels the pattern of Castro's more interesting career that it is impossible not to
see in *The Rover* further and unambiguous evidence for
Thomas Moser's conclusion that Conrad spent his last
years in a kind of fever of exhaustion, "rework[ing] old
materials." [51]

Though I am very far from arguing that Castro (or the
Dominic of the *Tremolino* story, for that matter) is one of
Conrad's most memorable creations, he is a far more convincing character than Peyrol and clearly (with Dominic)
Peyrol's original. Where Castro's conventional substance
is at least tempered with individual touches, Conrad's presentation of Peyrol is uncontaminated by imagination or
freshness. For this character Conrad has simply gathered
up the basic clichés of the type. He possesses, this "man of

violent deeds" (p. 23), an appropriately exotic and lawless
history: "the memories of his native country [were] overlaid by other memories . . . of endless oceans, . . . of
Arabs and negroes, . . . of fights at sea, rows on shore, desperate slaughter and desperate thirst" (p. 8). And he has,
this "rover of the outer seas" (p. 2), the required phy-
sique: "His bare torso thrown backwards and sustained by
his rigid big arms heavily tattooed on the white skin
above the elbows, Peyrol drew a long breath into his
broad chest with a pepper-and-salt pelt down the breast-
bone" (p. 12).

The embarrassingly awkward phrasing in this last sentence, a classic instance of what Moser calls the "sheer me-
chanical faultiness of the prose" in Conrad's late books,[52]
is, I should think, less disquieting than the tattoos and the
hairy chest. The obsession with vague physical details,
particularly with masculine profiles and broad chests
(compare Kurtz's spectral weakness or Giles's protruding
eyes in *The Shadow-Line*), in Conrad's last books is a decisive index of imaginative failure.

But in such physiques and in such men it is essential to
see the vestiges of much that is best and enduring in Conrad. The taciturn, heroic man of action may be a shocking
stereotype early and late in Conrad's career, but he has
more successful incarnations elsewhere in Conrad: in a
squadron of secondary characters like old Viola or Don
Pepe from *Nostromo;* in Captain MacWhirr from *Typhoon,* "tranquilly sure of himself" and "so sturdy of limb
that his clothes always looked a shade too tight for his
arms and legs" (pp. 3, 4); in Stein and the French Lieu-
tenant from *Lord Jim;* and, notably, in the figure of
Singleton aboard the *Narcissus,* especially near to the
stereotype—he is even tattooed—but superbly transcend-
ing the conventions out of which he was born to attain to
genuinely mythic stature:

> Alone in the dim emptiness of the sleeping forecastle he
> appeared bigger, colossal, very old; old as Father Time
> himself . . . He stood, still strong, as ever unthinking; a
> ready man with a vast empty past and with no future,
> with his childlike impulses and his man's passions already
> dead within his tattooed breast. The men who could un-
> derstand his silence were gone . . . They had been strong,
> as those are strong who know neither doubts nor hopes.
> They had been impatient and enduring, turbulent and
> devoted, unruly and faithful. . . . they had been men
> who knew toil, privation, violence, debauchery. [pp.
> 24–25]

It is worth observing parenthetically that the elevated diction in this passage, and especially the carefully balanced
pairs of adjectives in the next-to-last sentence, establish an
incantatory tone that is wholly appropriate to the mythic
figure being described: the note of ritual is not forced or
excessive here, as it frequently is elsewhere in Conrad's fiction, because the subject justifies, even requires, such elevation.

Conrad's success with Singleton illustrates one of the
two ways in which the dead clichés of the typical adventure character are enlivened in the major stories and novels. What Conrad does with Singleton and with the Dominic of the *Tremolino* story is consciously to exploit their
mythic or archetypal dimensions, delicately combining
references to their great size, strength, and skill with comparisons to older figures of legend and with reminders of
the long (and real as opposed to mythic) nautical history
of struggle and achievement that these men carry forward
and represent.

It is probable that Conrad wants us to recognize in Peyrol and in Tom Lingard of *The Rescue* something of the
mythic stature he successfully projects for Singleton, and
one can see, perhaps, how (for one example) Peyrol's

"Roman profile" (*The Rover,* p. 35) is intended to hint at epic qualities. But such qualities do not bear too much repeating, and they are reiterated beyond tolerable limits in the late novels. Aside from the faulty prose which mars the late books in which Peyrol and Lingard appear, Conrad's failure with these characters is surely in part a consequence of his decision to turn the tight-lipped Singleton-type into the protagonist. When such figures play secondary roles their radical lack of discrete human characteristics is unimportant and may even serve to emphasize the extent to which they represent, more grandly and powerfully than the ordinary sailor, a whole class of men. In addition, of course, their mythic stature can be suggested with a kind of economy scarcely possible when such figures become the focus of a long narrative: Peyrol and Lingard, that is to say, are unconvincing characters in part because the mythic or archetypal collapses back into stereotype when it is too much insisted upon.

Conrad's second way of retrieving freshness and life from the conventional materials of the typical adventure situation is, in a sense, the reverse of his first method. Where in the one case he will emphasize, even exaggerate, qualities that tend to be typical or representative, in the other case he will probe beneath the conventional surface to uncover its hidden individual and unique substance. To put the matter again: one method—that of his treatment of Singleton—is to force the stereotype to yield up its promise of the genuinely universal; the other method—that of his handling of Nostromo—is to contort the stereotype, to strike through it by recognizing and dramatizing what is seen to be the defining and unique integrity of this concretely rendered character or that fully explored situation. With the second method, undoubtedly the richer one though also the more difficult, Conrad will begin with the adventure cliché—Nostromo the indispen-

sable retainer, Jim the young sailor who must be tested—
but will refuse to rest in the simple expectations the convention encourages and will instead continually and
exhaustively insist on the character's discrete humanity,
on the event's concrete, *literal* truthfulness. With this second method Conrad is able to have it both ways. For behind his careful renderings of scene and character is a universe of hazard and adventure whose recurring appearance
in our dreams and fictions of escape and perilous
fraternity testifies to our need for it and imparts the resonance of myth, the whispered authority of fable, even to
Conrad's most concretely realized scenes and fully
rounded characters. Indeed, the full energies of the arche-
type are released only in the degree to which we can recognize the authoritative realism of a story's local details.
Because Conrad's major work always begins in such realism, his example argues the truth of Stevenson's defense of
adventure fiction far more persuasively than any book by
Stevenson himself:

> Novels thus begin to touch not the fine *dilettanti* but the
> gross mass of mankind, when they leave off to speak of
> parlours . . . and begin to deal with fighting, sailoring,
> adventure, death or child-birth. . . . These aged things
> have on them the dew of man's morning; they lie near,
> not so much to us, the semi-artificial flowerets, as to the
> trunk and aboriginal taproot of the race.[53]

Conrad's example, that is to say, justifies the essential
claims of this passage without committing itself to that
simplistic denial of the rational and the civilized which
here as elsewhere endangers Stevenson's good sense.

   Often in his variations on the adventure *bildungsroman*
Conrad will begin by explicitly invoking conventional expectations, and so will at once give us a measure of the
fullness and truthfulness of the story which is to follow,
even as he counts on the traditional notions to edge his

particular tale with intimations of the fabular. This is why Jim's untested illusions allow him "the hope of a stirring life in the world of adventure," a world he has conjured up from the conventional literary sources Conrad's novel itself intends to expose:

> On the lower deck in the babel of two hundred voices he would forget himself, and beforehand live in his mind the sea-life of light literature. He saw himself saving people from sinking ships, cutting away masts in a hurricane, swimming through a surf with a line; or as a lonely castaway, barefooted and half naked, walking on uncovered reefs in search of shell-fish to stave off starvation. He confronted savages on tropical shores, quelled mutinies on the high seas, and in a small boat upon the ocean kept up the hearts of despairing men—always an example of devotion to duty, and as unflinching as a hero in a book. [p. 6]

Jim has been reading Robert Louis Stevenson. Yet his imaginings are not so entirely repudiated as some readers may believe. For before his story is over Jim will indeed confront savages on tropical shores, will in his "pitiless wedding with a shadowy ideal of conduct" set an example of devotion at once courageous and egotistical, and will (ambiguously) earn the very adjective—*unflinching*—that in the beginning had described that make-believe hero in a book:

> The crowd, which had fallen apart behind Jim as soon as Doramin had raised his hand, rushed tumultuously forward after the shot. They say that the white man sent right and left at all those faces a proud and unflinching glance. Then with his hand over his lips he fell forward, dead. [p. 416]

The novel is a criticism of Jim's romantic fantasies, an anatomy of the cost of such fantasies, and in its responsible interest in motives and impulses gives us characters who are human beings and not the stick figures of the conventional adventure yarn. Yet for all of this, the events of the second half of the novel couldn't be more Stevensonian, and in what purports to be a realistic narrative—what *is* a realistic narrative—there exist lovely half-caste girls, brave native warriors, unscrupulous pirates, a mysterious suicide, exciting bloody battles, heroic death.

A systematic explanation for this paradox—for the fact, repeatedly true of Conrad's best fiction, that the most unpromising, recalcitrant, disruptively extravagant materials come to seem credible and worthy of the most serious attention—is the essential burden of chapter 4. But it is important here to stress the powerfully autobiographical character of Conrad's writing. Norman Sherry's recent investigations have remarkably extended our understanding of how intimately and precisely Conrad's fiction relies upon his own experiences, reading, and travel. In many instances, as Sherry and John Gordan have shown, Conrad's borrowings from his past are so exact as to be astonishing. Many of his characters bear names that are identical, or nearly so, with those of the living men on whom they are modeled, and Sherry is even able to provide us with a geographically accurate diagram of the path taken by one of Conrad's captains in his walks about Singapore.[54] This extreme literalism is clearly a definitive aspect of Conrad's temperament as a writer: not a virtue he sought but a limiting condition of his imagination and his sense of the world. It frequently finds disturbing expression in Conrad's prefaces, where an uneasy author keeps assuring us that his fiction is anchored in historical and personal actuality, and where even his richest and most innovative strategies seem to be understood with unsettling narrowness. In the preface to *Lord Jim,* for example, Conrad reconciles us to Marlow by observing that "some speeches in Parliament have taken nearer six than three hours in delivery" and by assuring us that despite the text's failure to mention "such insignificant details . . . there must have been refreshments on that night . . . to help the narrator on" (p. vii).

There is overwhelming evidence to suggest that the author of *Nostromo* was in thrall to a narrowly literal conception of fiction and that, as he himself acknowledged, his capacities for invention were dramatically circumscribed.[55] To perceive that Conrad was confined in such ways is to understand in yet another respect how specially menacing the mode of the adventure story was for him. Lacking the exuberant inventiveness of a writer like Dickens and temperamentally hostile to an expansive conception of fiction that might sanction, even encourage, allegory or fable, Conrad was caught in his own experiences and in his reverence for the actual.

Yet to acknowledge this, and to confront (as I have tried to do in this chapter) Conrad's inferior stories and novels, is not to disparage him but to value him more highly. Despite many unpersuasive particular judgments —he sees *Victory* and *Chance* as major successes, for example—the late Morton Zabel remains Conrad's greatest critic because his essays are continuously alive to the radical obduracy of Conrad's subject matter and of the alien language in which he wrote. "The world is too poor," Zabel splendidly says, "in writers who show us how it takes the whole strength and dedication of a lifetime to achieve literary endurance to permit us to minimize Conrad's example." [56]

Zabel is equally fine, I think, in his perception of the crucial fact that, as with all great writers, Conrad's very limitations are inextricably linked to his distinctive virtues. And this is particularly true of Conrad's attitude toward his rebellious subject matter:

> Conrad's material [Zabel writes] . . . came to him in
> terms the reverse of the aesthetic. It came to him as fact,
> as the data of serious and responsible experience. How-
> ever romantic or adventurous the emotion he took with
> him as a young man into the Merchant Service or the
> Orient, he knew those worlds first as worlds to be met
> and conquered by dint of hard labor, scrupulous industry,
> skill in the technique of his trade and cunning in his
> dealings with men. . . . His books issued from conditions
> as different as possible from those that produced the tales
> of Loti, Stevenson, or Maugham, all of them authors by
> profession, travelers by design, men who reconnoitered
> the exotic with express literary intention. Conrad is closer
> to such recent cases as those of Malraux, Saint-Exupéry,
> and George Orwell. He had to learn, know, and accept
> his subject matter on its own terms before he could see it
> in terms of art. When, years later, he came to make fiction
> of it, the integrity of the material acted as a discipline for
> the artist.[57]

The origins of Conrad's subjects were, then, essentially
nonliterary, and this is their great strength and value, particularly for a divided man like Conrad, an artist who profoundly distrusted the act of literature:

> The man of letters . . . often, especially in his youth, is
> inclined to lay a claim of exclusive superiority for his own
> amongst all the other tasks of the human mind. The mass
> of verse and prose may glimmer here and there with the
> glow of a divine spark, but in the sum of human effort it
> has no special importance. . . . To have the gift of words
> is no such great matter. ["Books," *Notes on Life and Let-
> ters,* pp. 7, 9]

These are the same doubts, elegantly contained, to
which Conrad gave more savage expression in his letters,
of which the following is a representative excerpt:

> It is a fool's business to write fiction for a living. . . .
> It is strange. The unreality of it seems to enter one's real

life, penetrate into the bones, make the very heartbeats
pulsate illusions through the arteries. One's will becomes
the slave of hallucinations, responds only to shadowy impulses, waits on imagination alone. A strange state, a
trying experience, a kind of fiery trial of untruthfulness.
And one goes through it with an exaltation as false as all
the rest of it. One goes through it,—and there's nothing
to show at the end. Nothing! Nothing! Nothing! [58]

If, as I will try to show in a later chapter, these very
doubts enrich Conrad's fiction, they also remind us that
Conrad's material was real for him in a particularly literal, and thus sustaining, way. This is especially true of
his treatment of the adventure partnership whose prototype is the relationship between Dominic Cervoni and the
young Conrad aboard the *Tremolino*. Speaking of Dominic in his author's note to *Nostromo,* Conrad makes this
revealing comment:

> He and I were engaged together in a rather absurd ad-
> venture, but the absurdity does not matter. It is a real sat-
> isfaction to think that in my very young days there must,
> after all, have been something in me worthy to command
> that man's half-bitter fidelity, his half-ironic devotion.
> [p. xx]

Explicit here is not only the adult Conrad's respect for
Dominic but also his pride in the callow adventurer who
risked measuring himself against such a man and on such
terms as that man chose.

Other, lesser writers in the same mode—Kipling, say,
or Rider Haggard, or Stevenson, whose treatment of one
version of the retainer figure anticipates Conrad's—turn
to the adventure partnership and to the type of the loyal
retainer because it is a literary convention, or because, ad-
ditionally, the abstract logic of their stories requires the
juxtaposition of their neophyte heroes against men of
more experience and achievement. But Conrad turns to

the convention out of much deeper causes: he turns to it not as literary formula or even imaginative insight, but as earned, lived truth—because that is the way it really happened to him and because he has in any case no other choice. For his deepest intuitions about the relations of men—intuitions whose sources include his orphaned childhood, his life-long ambivalence concerning his Polish heritage, his career as a seaman—press inescapably toward variations and reenactments of a single drama: a drama of generations in which youth and age play out a complex ritual of mutual hostility and dependence. Because this is so, Conrad's reliance on the adventure partnership and his recurring interest in tests and initiations retain a freshness and a conviction that distinguish him fundamentally from other writers for whom these things are merely *literary* truths, near-clichés, weary formulas. What Conrad makes of the convention depends, of course, on his artist's skill and intelligence. But the integrity with which he begins the act of art is a legacy of his experience as a man.

3   The Autobiographies

Conrad's *A Personal Record* (1912) deserves a more robust fame. Written in his phase of fullest mastery—it was first published in 1908–09 in Ford's *English Review*—this undervalued autobiographical memoir is a cunning paradigm of Conrad's impressionism. Remarkable in itself, the book offers also a clarifying demonstration of the way in which Conrad's first-person method can chasten a potentially extravagant subject matter, and—in the very performance of that task—can press toward intimate disclosures that richly dramatize his sense of the world.

That in *A Personal Record* Conrad abjures the right to invent scarcely eliminates the danger of grandiloquence or the more general danger of romanticizing either his own exploits or those of his grand-uncle Nicholas B., whose martial nobility is a prominent subject in the book. But it is true that the nonfictional substance of the memoir serves in some degree to minimize these dangers. This is so essentially because Conrad's tendency to heroic elevation collides here with his equally strong impulse to reticence about his personal and especially his inner life. "The matter in hand," he says explicitly, "is to keep these reminiscences from turning into confessions, a form of literary activity discredited by Jean Jacques Rousseau" (*Record*, pp. 94–95). And, indeed, some of Conrad's critics have commented somewhat testily on the book's refusal to give an account of its subject in the manner of conventional autobiographies.[1]

We know Conrad had a very different book in mind when he began these reminiscences, and it is significant

that *A Personal Record* diverges fundamentally from the
work Conrad described to his literary agent, James
Pinker, in October 1908, two months before the first in-
stallment of his memoirs appeared in Ford's magazine:

> I am anxious in other ways as to the *Rem^ces*. To
> make Polish life enter English literature is no small
> ambition—to begin with. But I think it can be done. To
> reveal a very particular state of society, bring forward in-
> dividuals with very special traditions and touch in a per-
> sonal way upon such events, for instance, as the liberation
> of the serfs (which in the number of people affected and
> in the general humanitarian significance is a greater fact
> of universal interest than the abolition of Negro Slavery)
> is a big enterprise. And yet it presents itself easily just be-
> cause of the intimate nature of the task, and of the 2 vols.
> of my uncle's *Memoirs* which I have by me, to refresh my
> recollections and settle my ideas. I can safely say that I
> feel equal to the work.[2]

The actual book largely ignores the promises of this synopsis; there is no extended discussion of the liberation of
the serfs, no serious attempt to make Polish culture accessible to English readers, and the Polish material that is present is entirely subordinated to the private, subjective intentions of the whole. Later in the same letter, instructing
Pinker about what to tell interested publishers, Conrad
mentions an aim we can still recognize in the finished
book, though here, too, the original intention has been
dramatically altered:

> You may say also that in the course of development the
> inner story of most of my books will come out—a sort of
> literary confession as to the sources as well as to the aims.
> I have been even thinking of a title something like: *The
> Art and the Life,* or *The Pages and the Years,* reminis-
> cences.

Ultimately, though with an obliqueness Conrad himself could not have anticipated, *A Personal Record* does indeed offer "the inner story" promised here. But except for *Almayer's Folly,* neither the origins nor the aims of any Conrad book is much discussed in the memoir, and about most of his work Conrad says nothing at all. Although all writers change their ideas in the act of writing, and although some alter their initial plans decisively, Conrad remains, if not unique, at least highly unusual in the extent to which he has departed from his first intentions in this volume of memoirs. And what is true of the development of *A Personal Record* is true also of Conrad's procedures in much of his fiction: the distance between original aim and final achievement is so great as to obscure almost entirely the book's origins. Not that this is cause for dissatisfaction, especially as regards *A Personal Record.* I think, in fact, that quite the reverse is true: that readers of Conrad should be grateful for the apparently diminished scope and ambitiousness of the book we have. For with the diminution has come tact, control, unity of tone; and without this serviceable modesty it is easy to imagine a book that would have been fragmentary and pretentious. (This imaginary book is rather less conjectural than one might think: it resembles in many essentials *The Mirror of the Sea.*) Simply to compare the final titles—the first English edition had been called *Some Reminiscences*—with Conrad's provisional suggestions is to confront in small the pretentious excess inherent in Conrad's first impulses for the memoir. As it got smaller, the book got better: became, in fact, as Albert Guerard has said, "one of Conrad's most subtly and most deliberately constructed books." [3]

Indeed, nothing in all of Conrad is more effortlessly complex in its management of chronology than part 4 of

A Personal Record (pp. 68–89). The section opens in
Uncle Tadeusz's home in Kiev, where Conrad visited during the 1890s, accompanied by the unfinished manuscript
of *Almayer's Folly*. Within one page we have retreated in
time and space to Conrad's rooms in London on the
morning in which he wrote the first lines of that novel.
Then, again within a page, we are carried yet further into
the past, into Conrad's childhood, where with his exiled
father he reads his first books, including his father's translation of *Two Gentlemen of Verona*. This reference leads
naturally, even inescapably, to the next major chronological jump—to Conrad's young manhood as a sailor in Fal-
mouth in the year of the bad gales, when he purchased his
five-shilling volume of Shakespeare, a random detail of immense implicit significance that links Conrad the seafarer
with two other writers-in-exile: his father and the author
of *Lord Jim*. The next shift returns us to the morning of
Almayer's birth; and then, in a final leap in time, part 4
concludes with Conrad's brilliantly dramatized account of
his meeting with the real-life Almayer in the Far East, a
passage of sustained characterization and vivid scenic effects that surpasses anything in *Almayer's Folly* itself.[4]
And of course, as with *Lord Jim* or *Nostromo,* this sequence enumerates only the major divisions, within which
there is still further disruption of normal chronological
order. The entire section, like the whole of the book, is a
marvel of delicacy but also of control, responsive to the
swift random logic of association and memory yet simultaneously obedient to the controlling themes of exile and
travel and the making of literature: an emblem finally for
Conrad's tangled potent intuition of how strangely
coherent—how enriched by continuity and how burdened
—are the discrete episodes of our individual lives.

Again, there are a number of anecdotes and stories in
the memoir as fine as anything in the fiction, vignettes in

which vividly created characters live for an instant in surroundings that are evoked with economy and precision: the story of Jacques, Conrad's first reader, who aboard the *Torrens* examined the unfinished manuscript of *Almayer's Folly* and who gave Conrad's apprentice writing his laconic encouragement; the story of the sacking of Nicholas B.'s residence by a greedy mob, an episode notable for the way in which Conrad turns Marlovian narrator, inventing dialogue and naming his sources for what he is recounting at second-hand ("I follow here the tale as told afterwards by the servant to my grand-uncle's friends and relatives, and as I have heard it repeated," p. 58); the evocation of the real-life Almayer; the dramatized scenes of Conrad's three examinations for officer's credentials in the British merchant navy, scenes whose dialogue is as fine as any Conrad ever wrote and whose fundamental substance casts back to *The Nigger of the "Narcissus"* and forward to *The Shadow-Line* ("this examiner . . . had given me an insight into his existence, awakening in me the sense of the continuity of that sea-life into which I had stepped from the outside . . . I felt adopted. His experience was for me . . . as though he had been an ancestor," p. 118).

The chief source of the book's grace and distinction is Conrad's narrative strategy, his decision to tell his story in slightly literary but nonetheless conversational accents, and to tell it in his characteristically evasive, dodging manner. The style that is a consequence of this strategy is profoundly self-conscious and is reluctant, often perhaps *unable,* to establish priorities in what it discusses. That is, at any given moment the defining subjectivity of this style is likely to discover the necessity of very concrete and precise evocation; it is likely to discover new interests, important nuances, that refuse to be ignored. In the largest sense, this means that however much Conrad may have intended to discuss the liberation of the serfs or Polish culture when he thought abstractly about his book, the act of writing it—the self-conscious, subjective indirections of his style—continually pressed away from such grandiose and public subjects toward those smaller but also truer subjects which touched his own experiences and preoccupations. Something very like this movement from easy and pretentious abstraction to small but concrete truth must likewise explain what happened to Conrad's initial conceptions for *Lord Jim* and *Heart of Darkness;* and it surely explains how *Under Western Eyes* evolved out of *Razumov,* the embarrassing love melodrama that Conrad earnestly described in a letter to Galsworthy and that we must be grateful he did not write.[5]

The first-person method in *A Personal Record,* then, as in much of Conrad's fiction, is a crucial source of discipline, is the enemy of pretentiousness. Yet even as it enforces such discipline, the style is not afraid to risk itself against those very elements it is designed to control. In *A Personal Record* Conrad avoids melodrama without surrendering the truly dramatic, he communicates his passion and his seriousness without sounding phony or leadenly portentous. It is a great feat, especially for a writer who was naturally prone to grandiloquence and exaggeration; and the evidence for it can be found in nearly every paragraph of *A Personal Record.* Here is Conrad generalizing about his impulse to write:

> I did not receive my visitors [the remembered figures of Almayer and company] with boisterous rapture as the bearers of any gifts of profit or fame. There was no vision of a printed book before me as I sat writing at that table, situated in a decayed part of Belgravia. After all these years, each leaving its evidence of slowly blackened pages, I can honestly say that it is a sentiment akin to piety which prompted me to render in words assembled with

conscientious care the memory of things far distant and
of men who had lived. [pp. 9–10]

Moments like this, moments in which Conrad (or his narrator) leaves off describing the specific scene or event and
begins to generalize from it, are frequently fatal for this
novelist, even in his best books. Yet here he succeeds completely. In spite of the largeness of its claim, the final sentence avoids the oracular portentousness to which Conrad
was prone in such circumstances. That long sentence,
thrusting as it does past several natural stopping places,
reproduces the authentic Conradian voice; its essential el-
ement, the literary virtue Conrad himself most highly val-
ued, is an utterly convincing sincerity.

That sincerity even survives the moments in which
Conrad tries to sound whimsical, a very surprising fact indeed when (with Morton Zabel) we recall that "the best
part of his talent was never casual, easygoing, haphazard,
or self-confident," when we realize that Conrad nearly always fails badly "in his moments of jocosity, self-conscious
humor, or decorous badinage." [6] A glance at Conrad's efforts in this direction in the critical and semi-autobiographical essays in *Notes on Life and Letters* confirms such a
judgment unarguably. But in *A Personal Record* Conrad
achieves at times a semi-whimsical tone which rings absolutely true and which, more importantly, undercuts the
visible temptations of oversolemnity:

> I knew, at a very early age, that my grand-uncle Nicholas
> B. was a Knight of the Legion of Honour and that he
> had also the Polish Cross for valour, *Virtuti Militari*. The
> knowledge of these glorious facts inspired in me an ad-
> miring veneration; yet it is not that sentiment, strong as it
> was, which resumes for me the force and the significance
> of his personality. It is overborne by another and complex
> impression of awe, compassion and horror. Mr. Nicholas

> B. remains for me the unfortunate and miserable (but he-
> roic) being who once upon a time had eaten a dog. [p.
> 32]

The tone here seems to me deceptively complex. The
grand, mouth-filling adjectives get their come-uppance in
the simplicity of the final eight words, and the entire passage shades quite delicately into self-mockery. Grand-uncle
Nicholas is not being satirized; but the man who is telling
this story is. The shift in focus away from Nicholas, the ostensible subject of the passage, toward the narrator himself is continued a few paragraphs later, where Conrad
subtly balances his mockery against his qualified seriousness without compromising either attitude:

> I have lived on ancient salt junk, I know the taste of
> shark, of trepang, of snake, of nondescript dishes contain-
> ing things without a name—but of the Lithuanian village
> dog never! I wish it to be distinctly understood that it is
> not I, but my grand-uncle Nicholas, of the Polish landed
> gentry, *Chevalier de la Légion d'Honneur,* etc. etc., who,
> in his young days, had eaten the Lithuanian dog.
> I wish he had not. . . . Still, if he really had to, let us
> charitably remember that he had eaten him on active ser-
> vice, while bearing up bravely against the greatest mili-
> tary disaster of modern history, and, in a manner, for the
> sake of his country. . . . *Pro patria!*
> Looked at in that light it appears a sweet and decorous
> meal. [pp. 34–35]

In the very next lines the tone alters drastically, abjur-
ing any hint of irony and brushing in dead earnest as near
to confession and explicit self-justification as Conrad will
ever come in his published writings:

> And looked at in the same light, my own diet of *la
> vache enragée* appears a fatuous and extravagant form of
> self-indulgence; for why should I, the son of a land which

such men as these have turned up with their ploughshares and bedewed with their blood, undertake the pursuit of fantastic meals of salt junk and hard tack upon the wide seas? On the kindest view it seems an unanswerable question. Alas! I have the conviction that there are men of unstained rectitude who are ready to murmur scornfully the word desertion. Thus the taste of innocent adventure may be made bitter to the palate. . . . No charge of faithlessness ought to be lightly uttered. . . . The inner voice may remain true enough in its secret counsel. The fidelity to a special tradition may last through the events of an unrelated existence. [pp. 35–36]

These lines are of importance because they illustrate with special clarity one of the seminal advantages of Conrad's narrative method, an advantage whose full value is evident only in the great first-person novels but whose essential character may be recognized rather more easily in this purer autobiographical context, where the distractions and wider claims of fiction are not present. What the lines show is the variety of tones open to Conrad when his narrative voice is that of a first-person speaker who claims his freedom from a consecutive chronology and whose decisions about what he shall discuss, and when, are (apparently) not strictly decisions at all, but are instead the subjective result of the unfettered play of his memories, impressions and feelings. And the lines show not simply that such variety is possible, but that it is possible within a very narrow compass, within the same chapter, section, page, even paragraph. The passage just quoted—serious, untouched by whimsy or the half-comic—asks, almost pleads, for the reader's sympathy and moral generosity, and with an earnestness that is wholly absent from the urbane self-criticism of the immediately preceding paragraphs. Although Conrad's great facility makes this shift in tone seem natural and even inevitable, it would be a mistake to imagine that such transitions are the result of anything less than high art. That art consists mainly in the success with which Conrad persuades us that whatever seems relevant to him is in fact relevant. There is really only the most tenuous of connections between the anecdote about an old soldier who was compelled to eat Lithuanian dog and Conrad's guilty sense that his departure from Poland came near to betrayal. But the connection suggested itself to the narrating mind that is the true subject of this book, and so the sharp transition from delicate half-mockery to earnest, nervous self-defense comes to seem entirely appropriate. In *Lord Jim* and *Heart of Darkness,* Marlow will be driven into precisely such transitions; and like Conrad in this passage from *A Personal Record,* he will reveal the extent to which he is himself judged and threatened by the actions of the man who is the ostensible subject of his story.

In the passage just quoted Conrad is attempting to confront the moral and emotional issues embodied for him in what he called "the only case of a boy of my nationality and antecedents taking a . . . standing jump out of his racial surroundings and associations" (*Record,* p. 121). But if his style chastens extravagance, it also protects him, or appears to protect him, from material that is too intimate and too painful. Several times in the book Conrad veers toward the question of his departure from Poland, and each time he shies away from decisive recognitions.[7] The technical adroitness which allows him to carry off such evasions is tested most fully in the paragraph that immediately follows the passage in which Conrad asserts that "fidelity to a special tradition may last through the events of an unrelated existence": "It would take too long to explain the intimate alliance of contradictions in human nature which makes love itself wear at times the desperate shape of betrayal" (p. 36). *It would take too long.* What

Conrad means, though we cannot charge him with conscious dissimulation, is that it would be too painful and
too difficult. So instead, with his unrivaled talent for sudden alterations in tone and in actual subject, Conrad
glides into a half-humorous disquisition on Don Quixote,
that "sublime *caballero*" who (presumably like the young
Conrad) "was not a good citizen" (pp. 36, 37). And this al-
lusive pleasantry leads Conrad—whose casual, jocular
tone has by now fully recovered itself, having escaped the
pressures of true self-examination—back into his own
past, to the time when his tutor, vacationing with Conrad
in central Europe, finally gave up in his attempt to dis-
courage Conrad's plans to go to sea, and signaled his sur-
render by calling his student an incorrigible Don Quixote.

No section of the book more clearly illustrates the
consummate subtlety of Conrad's narrative method. Having concluded his discussion of Don Quixote with the sentence, "But he was not a good citizen," Conrad supplies
the following transition: "Perhaps that and nothing more
was meant by the well-remembered exclamation of my
tutor" (p. 37). Then follows the story of the holiday, during the course of which Conrad dilates on the beauties of
the central European landscape, offers a detailed description of an Alpine hotel, and provides a lengthy portrait of
the Scottish tunnel engineer, who, except for tourists, was
Conrad's "first contact with British mankind" (p. 39).
Running through the episode is the tantalizing promise of
the tutor's "well-remembered exclamation." For all its
shifting and dodging, the episode seems bent on working
itself toward those words, and several times Conrad crypti-
cally reminds us of "the remark alluded to." When the remark finally comes—"You are an incorrigible, hopeless
Don Quixote. That's what you are"—its very postponement has invested it with enormous weight, and its appar-

ent connection to Conrad's earlier comments about "the ingenious hidalgo of La Mancha" surrounds it with the aura of revelation.

Yet like the deferred climaxes and artful postponements of his creature Marlow, Conrad's anecdote appears to frustrate our desire for decisive illumination. For although the analogy between the young Pole who went to sea and Don Quixote may in some sense describe the boy's innocent yearning for adventure, it scarcely probes seriously the themes of betrayal and loyalty which whisper (so Conrad unwillingly hints) in the dark ambiguities of this man's decision to leave his homeland.

It is the genius of *A Personal Record* finally to expose and to clarify those ambiguities not in its manifest content but in the subtle, immensely revealing drama of its form. First, the very evasiveness of the style—its preoccupation with concrete details, its impulse to elaboration and digression, its reluctance to conclude—constitutes a rich submerged drama of approach and withdrawal that deflects our attention from the younger self about whom Conrad is writing and toward the moral unease with which the older writer is privately contending. It is precisely such strategies of evasion that Conrad's narrators discover they must use. And as with those tellers, we measure Conrad's involvement in his story by the intensity and fullness of his tactics of postponement and indirection.

Beyond this, because Conrad's fidelity to his impressionistic method is wholly authentic—because, that is to say, the self's preoccupations genuinely direct the narrative— his first-person telling comes in the end to a clear if oblique confrontation with the very problems it has been driven to evade. This truly autobiographical style knows and dramatizes the central theme of *Lord Jim* and *Under Western Eyes:* there is ultimately no sanctuary from oneself. In the extended account of Conrad's holiday with his tutor, for example, the real analogy, the true connection, is not that between the young Conrad and Don Quixote, but the far more revealing parallel between the tutor who reluctantly sanctions Conrad's choice of life and grand-uncle Nicholas, the dead ancestor whose patriotic example, pages earlier, had awakened Conrad's guilt. Nicholas cannot, and probably would not, give his blessing to the nephew's commitment to exile; and so the tutor serves as his surrogate, a surrogate for the whole weight of those personal and cultural traditions that press far more heavily on the older writer, remembering but also evading his past, than on the younger self about whom he is writing.

A digression that refuses, finally, to digress, the story of Conrad's Alpine idyll is an emblem for the whole of *A Personal Record.* For in the anecdote itself as in the entire book, Conrad's first-person telling is afflicted by an inescapable, a radical candor. Imparting to every page and paragraph—almost to every sentence—a vital nervous energy, this fierce candor declares itself openly in recurring scenes whose burden is to disclose Conrad's deepest needs and uncertainties. These scenes unify his great autobiography and in a larger sense may be said to unify the world of his fiction. Their common subject is the precarious interdependence of men.

Sometimes, as in the account of Conrad's European holiday and in many episodes in the fiction, the scene focuses on youth's need to liberate itself from the confinements of authority and tradition. But elsewhere, and just as often —as, for example, in the episodes in *A Personal Record* concerning Conrad's examinations for his certification as a ship's officer or his encounter with the real Almayer— these confrontations between youth and age dramatize the complex, ambivalent mingling of affection, condescension, and vulnerable dependence that is awakened in older men in their dealings with the young. Finally, in many of its versions this archetypal Conradian situation will elaborate the subtle related impulse of the young to seek the approval of their elders. Conrad's young men, in the autobiographical works and in the fiction, fear and resist but also venerate the authority of age, experience, publicly acknowledged achievement. *Lord Jim* and *Under Western Eyes* are perhaps Conrad's most extended and probing treatments of this impulse, the protagonists of both books being driven repeatedly into confrontations with a variety of fathers and elders, their behavior a riddling mixture of abasement and self-assertion.[8] But the anecdote in *A Personal Record* (pp. 15–18) that recounts Conrad's "sudden impulse" to ask a stranger to read the unfinished manuscript of his first novel is also a particularly rich enactment of this last version of Conrad's fundamental scene.

The manuscript, Conrad tell us, "got carried for three years to and fro upon the sea" during his days as a sailor. His wavering commitment to the act of writing ebbs during these years until it "became at last unreasonable to suppose that anything in the world would ever happen to Almayer and Nina." Then, as so often in Conrad's fiction, the young man's uncertainties and sense of aloneness are mitigated by an instant of companionship:

> Providence which saved my MS. from the Congo rapids brought it to the knowledge of a helpful soul far out on the open sea. It would be on my part the greatest ingratitude ever to forget the sallow, sunken face and the deepset, dark eyes of the young Cambridge man (he was a "passenger for his health" on board the good ship *Torrens* outward bound to Australia) who was the first reader of "Almayer's Folly"—the very first reader I ever had. "Would it bore you very much reading a MS. in a handwriting like mine?" I asked him one evening on a sudden impulse at the end of a longish conversation whose sub-

ject was Gibbon's History. Jacques (that was his name) was sitting in my cabin one stormy dog-watch below, after bringing me a book to read from his own travelling store.

"Not at all," he answered with his courteous intonation and a faint smile.

Jacques comes to Conrad's cabin on the following day and silently returns the manuscript. In the marvelously understated scene that follows we watch Conrad hesitantly asking this literary stranger to sanction his impulse to write novels. The scene emphasizes especially the enormous distance between this Polish ship's officer and an aristocratic Englishman whose health is failing. That Jacques's encouragement is minimal, perhaps no more than reluctant courtesy, and that the apprentice writer must labor to draw it out, is part of the scene's brilliant truthfulness.

"Well, what do you say?" I asked at last. "Is it worth finishing?" This question expressed exactly the whole of my thoughts.

"Distinctly," he answered in his sedate veiled voice, and then coughed a little.

"Were you interested?" I inquired further, almost in a whisper.

"Very much!"

Now follows a long paragraph in which Conrad describes the cabin in which this drama of qualified communion is taking place. The ship rolls heavily; there is a "prolonged silence." Then Conrad speaks again.

"Now let me ask you one more thing: Is the story quite clear to you as it stands?"

He raised his dark, gentle eyes to my face and seemed surprised.

"Yes! Perfectly."

This was all I was to hear from his lips concerning the merits of "Almayer's Folly." . . . When we arrived at Adelaide the first reader of my prose went at once up-country, and died rather suddenly.

That our precarious connections with others occur unexpectedly and cannot endure, and that we are driven still to make and to find them, is the seminal intuition of this scene, of the splendid autobiographical testament in which it appears, and, as I will argue, of the whole of Conrad's work.

THE MIRROR OF THE SEA

The Mirror of the Sea (1906) is a far more casual performance than *A Personal Record,* and its defects are in consequence both clearer and more likely to inhibit one's appreciation of its substantial local successes. Less satisfying as a whole than *A Personal Record, The Mirror of the Sea* is also less cautious and more energetic. And for an understanding of Conrad's fiction and the attitudes that shape it, *The Mirror of the Sea* is arguably the more important book. Despite its deficiencies—and occasionally, in fact, *because* of them—this volume comes near to being the "very intimate revelation" (*Mirror,* p. v) its author claimed it was, although not entirely in the sense that he intended.

That *The Mirror* as a whole is uneven and fragmentary is beyond dispute. Even the early reviewer who hailed its publication as a "conspicuous" event and who praised the book lavishly found it necessary to express gentle misgivings about the essay on Nelson that Conrad tacked on at the end.[9] Although he apparently tried to impose some coherence on the book by arranging his chapters in a sequence different from the order of their appearance as magazine articles, Conrad did not succeed in obscuring the occasional and commercial nature of many of the book's separate parts. Two of those parts, in fact, "Overdue and Missing" and "The Grip of the Land" (pp. 56–70) were originally conceived as independent piece-work, unconnected with other articles written during the same period which Conrad intended for the volume that became *The Mirror of the Sea*.[10]

"I've started a series of sea sketches," he wrote to Wells in a typical gesture of self-laceration,

> and have sent out P[inker] on the hunt to place them. This must save me. I've discovered that I can dictate that sort of bosh without effort at the rate of 3,000 words in four hours. Fact. The only thing now is to sell it to a paper and then make a book of the rubbish. Hang![11]

Though hardly the "bosh" Conrad calls it here, much of *The Mirror* was obviously written only for money. There is a real and sustained coherence in only three sections of the book—"Initiation," "The Nursery of the Craft," and "The 'Tremolino' " (pp. 128–83)—and it is significant that the latter two chapters were never published in maga-zine form and were (presumably) written in sequence spe-cifically for the book. It is likely, also, that "Initiation," the only chapter of the memoir to be published as an arti-cle in the same year as the book's publication, was origi-nally composed as part of this final sequence.

That Ford helped Conrad to write significant portions of *The Mirror of the Sea* has never been doubted, but Arthur Mizener, in his recent biography of Ford, was the first to reveal that during the composition of the early sec-tions Conrad and Ford decided to make the book a formal collaboration.[12] Ford himself never says *The Mirror* origi-nated as a partnership, and it is important to recognize that this is an instance in which he seems to have been re-strained in his claims about his relation to Conrad's work.[13] Ford's contribution to *The Mirror of the Sea* is es-tablished in an unpublished letter from Conrad to Ford,

written nearly four months after Conrad announced to
Wells that he had begun "a series of sea sketches":

> I saw Pinker the other day. No word yet from [George
> B.] Harvey [editor of *Harper's Weekly*] as to sketches.
> [George Roland] Halkett [editor of the *Pall Mall Maga-
> zine*] offered to take *six* at £ 5.5 per thou[sand] *Eng.
> rights* but is being held off and meantime somebody else
> (?) is looking at them here with a view of trying for bet-
> ter terms. Halkett really is a last resource and I told
> P[inker] not to throw the thing away in haste. But
> still Halketts proposal means 90 gs of which (I told
> Pinker again) I must have 30 when—and if—the affair is
> concluded, pour Votre Seigneurie. As to the book form
> (which Harvey already is ready to take) a small calcu-
> lation will fix our proportions; for I suppose we can
> not now finish the whole together. Can we?[14]

Since the *Pall Mall Magazine* published five chapters of
the book (in six installments, all during 1905),[15] it would
appear that Pinker was unable to place the articles elsewhere. And because the letter mentions a firm offer from
Halkett, it seems safe to assume that the six articles that
were published in the magazine are the same sketches to
which Conrad is referring. This means that Ford's share
in the book is probably limited to these five chapters, not
all of which had to have been completed by the time of
Halkett's offer.

Jocelyn Baines quotes from this Conrad letter in his biography but, curiously, fails to conclude that the book
began as a collaboration.[16] The letter, however, seems to
make it clear that Ford and Conrad had agreed, formally
and explicitly, to write the book together, but that Conrad completed most of the book on his own when collaboration became impossible for unspecified reasons.[17] Since
Conrad made minute and fairly frequent alterations in
the magazine pieces when he published them as a book,

there is no question that he is fully responsible for every line in *The Mirror of the Sea*.[18] It is perhaps best to avoid speculation as to the precise extent of Ford's work on the book, and simply to acknowledge that his initial contribution must have been considerable enough to justify Conrad's concern "to fix our proportions" but not substantial enough to justify calling the book a collaboration.

The letter to Ford from which I have just quoted is focused, of course, on the question of payment, and reminds us again, like Conrad's earlier letter to Wells, of the fact that *The Mirror of the Sea* was conceived in a desperate effort to rescue its author from financial difficulties. The circumstances of its conception, then, its piecemeal growth, its aborted beginning as a collaboration, its intended appeal to a popular audience—all this helps to explain the book's fragmentary quality and makes it clear that when Conrad calls the work his "confession" in his author's note (p. vii), he is, to say the least, exaggerating.

He is exaggerating, too, though in the opposite direction, when he violently condemns the book in his letter to Wells. Far from a confession, even less is this book "rubbish": and only the faintest suggestion of overemphasis makes one wish to qualify Morton Zabel's judgment of *The Mirror of the Sea* as "an essential document on [Conrad's] life and thought." [19]

It is an essential document even in its worst aspects. This is particularly true of its lush prose, for the rhetoric of romantic excess that mars substantial portions of *The Mirror of the Sea* illustrates all too certainly how an unvigilant Conrad could fall into the pose of a bard of the adventurous life, whose cloying lyrics celebrate a phony and callow glamor:

> The end of the day is the time to gaze at the kingly face of the Westerly Weather, who is the arbiter of ships' des-

> tinies. Benignant and splendid, or splendid and sinister, the western sky reflects the hidden purposes of the royal mind. Clothed in a mantle of dazzling gold or draped in the rags of black clouds like a beggar, the might of the Westerly Wind sits enthroned upon the western horizon with the whole North Atlantic as a footstool for his feet and the first twinkling stars making a diadem for his brow. [*Mirror,* p. 81]

The trivial anthropomorphism here is not, alas, limited to a single paragraph or page but appears through long portions of *The Mirror of the Sea.* This is a book of which it can confidently be said that the excision of fully a third or more of its pages would constitute an aesthetic improvement.

Yet this gain would also render the book less valuable as a casebook of Conradian themes, attitudes and—most of all—weaknesses. Moreover, its very unevenness serves to make clear that while melodramatizing inclinations like those in the passage just quoted may constitute a serious threat to the integrity of Conrad's work, these same tendencies—controlled, chastened, but never completely eliminated—are also a source of real energy and artistic strength. The book, indeed, is an exemplary, even a crystallizing instance of the dangers but also the opportunities inherent in Conrad's use of materials deriving from the romantic side of his nature and from the conventions of the adventure tale.

If the sterile personifications that recur in such chapters as "The Character of the Foe" or "Rulers of East and West" are especially unconvincing, the same literary technique, and the same qualities of temperament that give birth to the technique, lie behind the chapter, "In Captivity," itself perhaps slightly overdone but engaging and serious in its way. Here is the opening paragraph:

A ship in dock, surrounded by quays and the walls of warehouses, has the appearance of a prisoner meditating upon freedom in the sadness of a free spirit put under restraint. Chain cables and stout ropes keep her bound to stone posts at the edge of a paved shore, and a berthing-master, with brass buttons on his coat, walks about like a weather-beaten and ruddy gaoler, casting jealous, watchful glances upon the moorings that fetter a ship lying passive and still and safe, as if lost in deep regrets of her days of liberty and danger on the sea. [p. 115]

This is authentic Conrad, the Conrad of *The Nigger of the "Narcissus"* and other later successes. And although the slight ornateness of the passage, the attention to rhythm, the adjectival and metaphoric emphasis, might cause discomfort for certain modern readers who have been taught to distrust such qualities in prose, I can only say, following Ian Watt,[20] that to reject this passage is to reject not only most of Conrad but a number of other major writers as well.

The clear superiority of the second passage scarcely requires lengthy illustration. What needs to be stressed is that the two passages do not issue from separate compartments of Conrad's brain but derive instead from roughly similar notions and feelings. That the vapid romanticizing of the first is offensively trivial while the strong current of nostalgia and heroic exaggeration in the second seems justified and even in some degree, moving—this is quite certainly a consequence of the rigor, both stylistic and intellectual, that Conrad brought to bear when he wrote the later passage. The rigor is responsible for the way in which the various concrete details—the quays, the warehouses, the chain cables, the berthing-master's buttons, the whole slight but real sense of *location*—chasten the potentially sentimental metaphor of the fettered ship.

And because of this rigor the paragraph accomplishes a
delicate task: avoiding false emotionalism, it yet celebrates
unashamedly the importance and the honest glamor of the
seafaring life. In its small way the paragraph enacts the
tribute Conrad wished to make "to the imperishable sea,
to the ships that are no more, and [this, by implication] to
the simple men who have had their day" (*Mirror,* p. viii).

Not all of what follows the opening paragraph is
equally successful. Conrad perhaps overextends the
prisoner-ship metaphor, and may insist too often on the
ship's feminine qualities—though it must be said that this
insistence has legitimate warrant in the vocabulary of the
nautical tradition whose ancient values the chapter and
the entire book are meant to invoke and to preserve. But
the lapses are slight, and Conrad's vision of the docked
ship, moored "on a dark, greasy, square pool of black water" as "the odious . . . shadows of walls and roofs fall
upon her decks, with showers of soot" (pp. 116, 117) recalls not dishonorably another and greater passage:

> The *Narcissus* came gently into her berth; the shadows of
> soulless walls fell upon her, the dust of all the continents
> leaped upon her deck, and a swarm of strange men, clam-
> bering up her sides, took possession of her in the name of
> the sordid earth. She had ceased to live. [*The Nigger of
> the "Narcissus,"* p. 165]

Though we must, indeed, turn to Conrad's first masterpiece in order to see him use in its fullest resonance this
sailor's vision of the land spoiling and degrading his ship,
Conrad's rendering of that vision in *The Mirror of the
Sea* has behind it considerable and even memorable
weight. And whatever weight, whatever truth inheres in
that vision is the direct, if qualified, expression of "the romantic feeling of reality" Conrad himself knew was a key
to his temperament (*Within the Tides,* p. v).

Other things, both good and bad, in *The Mirror of the Sea* lead just as directly into the fiction. The irrelevant eulogy on Nelson, overwritten, unqualified in its enthusiasm for the glamorous deed of war—"Other men there were ready and able to add to the treasure of victories the British navy has given to the nation. It was the lot of Lord Nelson to exalt all this glory. Exalt! the word seems to be created for the man" (p. 185)—prefigures the essential temper of such disappointing fiction as "Gaspar Ruiz," "The Duel" (1908), and *The Rover* (1923). In the final pages of Conrad's last-completed novel, in fact, Nelson himself makes a brief appearance and speaks the author's epitaph for old Peyrol:

> "But I am like that white-headed man you admire so much, Vincent," [Nelson] . . . pursued with a weary smile. "I will stick to my task till perhaps some shot from the enemy puts an end to everything." [pp. 275–76]

Indeed, the whole manner of Conrad's treatment of his story and his hero in *The Rover*, and particularly his sentimental handling of the final episode in which the English Captain Vincent sinks Peyrol's tartane and voices as he does so some empty pieties about the courage and worth of his adversary, merely attenuates the easy vaporings of the Nelson essay.

Similarly, Conrad's most ornately rhythmical invocations to the weather, the sea, and the art of sailing in *The Mirror of the Sea* seem to derive from the same region of feeling as such poor pieces as "Freya of the Seven Isles" (1912) and "The Planter of Malata" (1914), where the largely verbal excess of the autobiographical book is translated into a more damaging extravagance affecting not merely style but also plot and the conception of character.

Yet these weak moments in *The Mirror of the Sea* may have claims on us that are not simply negative. In the undistinguished chapter entitled "The Fine Art," for example, Conrad gives lucid expression to a conviction that is central to much that is fine in his fiction:

> Now, the moral side of an industry, productive or unproductive, the redeeming and ideal aspect of this bread-winning, is the attainment and preservation of the highest possible skill on the part of the craftsmen. Such skill, the skill of technique, is more than honesty; it is something wider, embracing honesty and grace and rule in an elevated and clear sentiment, not altogether utilitarian, which may be called the honour of labour. It is made up of accumulated tradition, kept alive by individual pride, rendered exact by professional opinion, and, like the higher arts, it is spurred on and sustained by discriminating praise.
>
> This is why the attainment of proficiency, the pushing of your skill with attention to the most delicate shades of excellence, is a matter of vital concern. [p. 24]

We need not disagree with Leavis when he insists that we distort Conrad if we limit him to a mere vocational ethic, nor with Irving Howe, who sees that Conrad's "famous 'job sense' " is often "a security *faute de mieux*," [21] in order to perceive in the passage just quoted a double relevance: to Conrad's sense of his craft as a writer and to the related preoccupation, clearest of course in the sea stories, with the value and saving power of work. "The seaman's instinct alone survived whole in my moral dissolution," says the narrator in *The Shadow-Line* (p. 109), echoing the Marlow of *Heart of Darkness* and *Lord Jim* and implicitly explaining the heroism of men like Singleton and MacWhirr.

Thus far I have been discussing *The Mirror of the Sea* as if it were a mere gloss on the fiction. But the book is more than that. In several of its episodes the memoir en-

gages certain of Conrad's recurring themes, stylistic problems, and human relationships with an independent
adroitness that compares favorably with the fiction itself.

In January 1902, more than two years before he began
writing *The Mirror of the Sea,* Conrad wrote to Meldrum
of his plans for the book:

> I am, as soon as ever I can, going to work for *Maga* at
> last. My idea is to do some autobiographical matter about
> Ships, skippers, and an adventure or two. How will that
> do? Pray tell me. *Youth* style upon the whole only not
> with the note of Youth in it but of the *wonderfulness* of
> things, events, people,—when looked back upon. . . . Of
> course it shall be "fiction" in the same sense that *Youth* is
> fiction.[22]

The comparison with "Youth" seems particularly apt, for
nostalgia is in a way the very subject of *The Mirror of the
Sea,* but nostalgia handled—I am speaking now of the
book's successful passages—rather more subtly than in
Conrad's first major short story. In both works Conrad's
point of view is that of an older remembering narrator
who treats his younger self with an affection tempered by
irony. But in "Youth" this irony is sometimes forced and
heavy-handed, and suggests that Conrad, newly met with
Marlow, though conscious of the need to correct the unre-
strained sentimentality that is potentially present in his
story, has not yet found a way to register sympathy and
judgment simultaneously. The result of such difficulties is
that Marlow's lament for his youth turns at times into an
empty-headed obviousness that is faintly reminiscent of
bad Wordsworth:

> O youth! The strength of it, the faith of it, the imagi-
> nation of it! To me [the *Judea*] was not an old rattle-
> trap carting about the world a lot of coal for a freight—
> to me she was the endeavour, the test, the trial of life. I

> think of her with pleasure, with affection, with regret—as
> you would think of someone dead you have loved. I
> shall never forget her. . . . Pass the bottle. [p. 12; ellipsis
> Conrad's]
>
> Ah! The good old time—the good old time. Youth and
> the sea. Glamour and the sea! The good strong sea, the
> salt, bitter sea, that could whisper to you and roar at you
> and knock your breath out of you. [p. 42]

There is simply no way in which a sensible criticism can
justify this kind of rhetoric. Leavis is right to object to the
story's "cheap insistence on the glamour." [23] And although
The Mirror of the Sea is tarred throughout with the same
sentimental brush, there is nothing in that book to match
the simplistic rib-nudging of the passages just quoted. In
the autobiographical episodes that are the core of *The
Mirror of the Sea* Conrad succeeds in communicating an
authentic nostalgia, and he does so with a grace that is,
for all its verbal ornament, more impressive than the shallow lyricism of "Youth." In a further contrast with the
sometimes crude irony that mars the early story, Conrad in
The Mirror qualifies his nostalgia with a wry, partly ironic
amusement that persuades the reader both of the worth of
the younger self whose adventures are being recounted and
of the maturity and intelligence of the older man who is
telling about them:

> The thing (I will not call her a ship twice in the same
> half-hour) leaked. She leaked fully, generously, overflow-
> ingly, all over—like a basket. I took an enthusiastic part
> in the excitement caused by that last infirmity of noble
> ships, without concerning myself much with the why or
> the wherefore. The surmise of my maturer years is that,
> bored by her interminable life, the venerable antiquity
> was simply yawning with ennui at every seam. But at the
> time I did not know; I knew generally very little, and
> least of all what I was doing in that *galère*. . . .

The truth must have been that, all unversed in the arts of the wily Greek, the deceiver of gods, the lover of strange women, the evoker of bloodthirsty shades, I yet longed for the beginning of my own obscure Odyssey, which, as was proper for a modern, should unroll its wonders and terrors beyond the Pillars of Hercules. The disdainful ocean did not open wide to swallow up my audacity, though the ship, the ridiculous and ancient *galère* of my folly, the old, weary, disenchanted sugar-wagon, seemed extremely disposed to open out and swallow up as much salt water as she could hold. This, if less grandiose, would have been as final a catastrophe. [pp. 153–54]

The nostalgia here is genuine, but so is the self-mockery; and these passages, like others in those parts of *The Mirror of the Sea* in which Conrad relates anecdotes from his sailing experience, are less tainted by the forced levity and by the general impression of artificiality that appears more than occasionally in "Youth."

As the last sentences in the passage just quoted indicate, the ironic note in the autobiographical portions of *The Mirror of the Sea* is not consistently effective. It falters, for example—and in a way that is fairly characteristic of Conrad's writing elsewhere—in the chapter entitled "Initiation." After a general prologue of some eight pages concerning the pride and faith of seamen in their ships and concluding with a typically grandiloquent passage celebrating the "impenetrable and heartless" cruelty of the sea, Conrad narrates the story of his rescue of the crew of a Danish brig that had foundered in the mid-Atlantic. The story is in large measure detachable from its context and can stand with something of the finished authority of the short fiction.[24] Like the account of the *Tremolino* adventure, the episode is a virtual catalogue of the themes and situations to which Conrad returns again and again in his fiction.

As the rescue boats are lowered, Conrad, who is to command one of the boats, is drawn aside by his captain:

> "You look out as you come alongside that she doesn't take you down with her. You understand?"
>
> He murmured this confidentially, so that none of the men at the falls should overhear, and I was shocked. "Heavens! as if in such an emergency one stopped to think of danger!" I exclaimed to myself mentally, in scorn of such cold-blooded caution.
>
> It takes many lessons to make a real seaman, and I got my rebuke at once. My experienced commander seemed in one searching glance to read my thoughts on my ingenuous face.
>
> "What you're going for is to save life, not to drown your boat's crew for nothing," he growled. [pp. 139–40]

In addition to the way in which Conrad in these lines unobtrusively makes us aware of the poised balance between the *then* of the adventure and the *now* of its telling, this passage promises one of those archetypal Conradian test situations and dramatizes Conrad's sense of a universe filled with decisive moments.

The young Conrad's scorn of "such cold-blooded caution" recalls Jim's "hope of a stirring life in a world of adventure" (*Lord Jim,* p. 6) and recalls, too, young Marlow's decision in "Youth" to outdistance the other longboats as the crew departs from the burning *Judea:* "I wanted to have my first command all to myself. I wasn't going to sail in a squadron if there were a chance for independent cruising" (p. 34).

In "Initiation" we are told in the end that the young Conrad's sudden recognition of the sea's malevolence utterly changes him, even though Conrad has earlier remarked that it takes many lessons to become a seaman:

> On that exquisite day of gentle breathing peace and veiled sunshine perished my romantic love to what men's

imagination had proclaimed the most august aspect of
Nature. . . . I saw the duplicity of the sea's most tender
mood. . . . In a moment, before we shoved off, I had
looked coolly at the life of my choice. Its illusions were
gone, but its fascination remained. I had become a seaman at last. . . .

It was not for [my captain] . . . to discern upon me
the marks of my recent initiation. And yet I was not exactly the same youngster who had taken the boat away.
[pp. 141, 148]

But readers of *The Shadow-Line* may well be permitted
to wonder whether any single event can be so weighty,
and to suspect, indeed, that a belief in such decisive possibilities is itself a romantic illusion. This suspicion is
strengthened by the grandiloquence that accompanies
Conrad's description of the "true" ocean as opposed to the
"false" one of his boyish dreams:

Already I looked with other eyes upon the sea. I knew
it capable of betraying the generous ardour of youth as
implacably as, indifferent to evil and good, it would have
betrayed the basest greed or the noblest heroism. My conception of its magnanimous greatness was gone. And I
looked upon the true sea—the sea that plays with men
till their hearts are broken, and wears stout ships to
death. Nothing can touch the brooding bitterness of its
soul. Open to all and faithful to none, it exercises its fascination for the undoing of the best. To love it is not well.
It knows no bond of plighted troth, no fidelity to misfor-
tune, to long companionship, to long devotion. The
promise it holds out perpetually is very great; but the
only secret of its possession is strength, strength—the jealous, sleepless strength of a man guarding a coveted treasure within his gates. [p. 148]

Impressively phrased as much of this is, the pathetic fal-
lacy gives Conrad away. This lush rhetoric partly

undermines his claim that, having looked on the life of
his choice, he discovered on that bright morning that "its
illusions were gone."

Conrad is rather more convincing in "Initiation" with
another theme which, like the test situation itself, is at the
very center of nearly all of his fiction:

> We could not . . . have picked out a better day for our
> regatta had we had the free choice of all the days that
> ever dawned upon the lonely struggles and solitary ag-
> onies of ships since the Norse rovers first steered to the
> westward against the run of the Atlantic waves. [p. 140]

Though the reference to the Norse rovers seems simply to
reinforce the story's exotic qualities, it has, I think, a
more serious function, for in its slight way the reference
calls attention to the fact that what Conrad and his crew
are doing has been done in the same way many times before over many centuries: the sentence thus invokes a
whole tradition of common struggle and common labor
which places the specific moment Conrad is describing in
a context that universalizes and dignifies it. The same
thing occurs a few pages later, where Conrad reminds us
that the captain he has just rescued is a "descendant of the
most ancient sea-folk," whose sad smile as his brig disap-
pears beneath the sea expresses "an infinite depth of he-
reditary wisdom" (p. 147).

Repeatedly in *The Mirror of the Sea* Conrad deepens
in just this way the theme of personal nostalgia by insist-
ing on the larger, communal implications of his connection with the seafaring life. And it is this recurring assertion of his typicality, of the extent to which his
experiences and responses at sea have been shared by
many other human beings, which most significantly links
the autobiographical volume with Conrad's best fiction,

and which, together with its statement in the fiction, defines one of Conrad's enduring qualities. As Ian Watt has
helped us to see,

> Many things in himself, his life and his times, gave him
> as deep a sense of the modern alienation as any other of
> our great exiled and isolated writers; and yet Conrad's
> most vigorous energies were turned away from the ever-
> increasing separateness of the individual and towards
> discovering values and attitudes and ways of living and
> writing which he could respect and yet which were, or
> could be, widely shared. . . . In the centrality of his ul-
> timate purpose Conrad is akin to Wordsworth.[25]

A key aspect of that purpose is plain, and often memora-
bly stated, in *The Mirror of the Sea,* and even goes some
way toward justifying in principle if not in execution such
chapters as "The Heroic Age" or "Rulers of East and
West"—chapters which pay only abstract tribute to the
shared dangers and the shared history of the seafaring adventure. Whatever unity *The Mirror of the Sea* may be
said finally to possess—and its parts, indeed, do reach toward a theoretical harmony which carries a real if limited
conviction—is a direct consequence of the long historical
and communal perspective that is consistently invoked in
passages like the following:

> The cradle of oversea traffic and of the art of naval
> combats, the Mediterranean, apart from all the associa-
> tions of adventure and glory, the common heritage of all
> mankind, makes a tender appeal to a seaman. It has shel-
> tered the infancy of his craft. He looks upon it as a man
> may look at a vast nursery in an old, old mansion where
> innumerable generations of his own people have learned
> to walk. I say his own people because, in a sense, all sail-
> ors belong to one family: all are descended from that ad-
> venturous and shaggy ancestor who, bestriding a shapeless

> log and paddling with a crooked branch, accomplished
> the first coasting trip in a sheltered bay ringing with the
> admiring howls of his tribe. [pp. 148–49]

> The seaman of the last generation, brought into sympathy
> with the caravels of ancient time by his sailing-ship, their
> lineal descendant, cannot look upon those lumbering
> forms navigating the naive seas of ancient woodcuts with-
> out a feeling of surprise, of affectionate derision, envy, and
> admiration. For those things, whose unmanageableness,
> even when represented on paper makes one gasp with a
> sort of amused horror, were manned by men who are his
> direct professional ancestors. [p. 72]

The pieties so delicately expressed here explain the intensity and the seriousness of Conrad's lament for the passing
of the sailing fleet.[26] Conrad's sailors, descended from
Norse rovers and Elizabethan adventurers, have inherited
the same struggle, are visited by the same catastrophes,
and survive by essentially the same exercise of skill and
vigilance. Conrad's distaste for steam is not, therefore, a
mere reactionary whim but follows from his recognition
that steam-powered vessels have altered the relationship
between the sailor and his ship and appear to threaten the
tradition of common danger which weds the modern seaman to the remote past of his profession. There is a sense
in which Conrad is thus protesting against the decline of
the artisan—"The machinery, the steel, the fire, the steam
have stepped in between the man and the sea" (p. 72)—
and it is not, perhaps, inappropriate to observe that such
sentiments have an honorable place in that impressive
body of Victorian and Edwardian prose whose response to
the implacable man-denying pressures of the industrial
revolution is a *cri de coeur* which seems in our era both
prophetic and a good deal more compelling than the
graceless objectivities of the sociological survey.

The communal and historical perspective celebrated in

the passages quoted above is always present in the specific personal events Conrad narrates in *The Mirror of the Sea.* And it is that perspective which sanctions in Conrad's writing, as it does not, for example, in the work of Stevenson, a reliance on the themes and situations of the common adventure tale. The dangers and excitements and tests that Conrad's seamen undergo, in *The Mirror of the Sea* no less than in *Lord Jim,* are distinguished fundamentally from Stevensonian adventures because Conrad's recurring invocation of the historical context reveals that his interests are serious and moral: far from claiming that such dangers are unique, far from aiming to shock his readers with the strangeness of the life he describes, Conrad sees and wants his readers to see that these dangers are, in fact, ordinary and common; that they define a continuity of human struggle and achievement; that, finally, the circumstances of the seafaring life can suggest by implication some of the essential conditions of the larger human community.

Though Conrad uses generalizing paragraphs that speak explicitly about the seafaring inheritance to place his personal experience in the context of an ancient tradition, his interest in this theme goes beyond such abstraction and is realized dramatically, as in the sea fiction, in the relationships between young seamen and their more experienced elders. Those relationships—between the young Conrad and his various captains, between Conrad and the first-mate Mr. B., most significantly in *The Mirror* between Conrad and Dominic Cervoni, *padrone* of the *Tremolino*—enact a ritual of continuity, dramatize the theme of solidarity and human dependence about which other passages in *The Mirror of the Sea* speak only abstractly.

This vision of communion between youth and experience is rendered the more compelling because of the way

in which Conrad's formal design contributes to his theme.
For in *The Mirror of the Sea* Conrad's narrative voice, at
once affectionate and ironic, joins him as author to the
company of experienced seniors with whom his younger
self is associated in the past his book recreates. Presenting
a simultaneous view of the young man who acts out the
story and of the older self who tells about it, the narrative
strategy itself embodies the juxtaposition of youth and
age, of past and present, which is the essential theme of
The Mirror of the Sea in both its personal and its historical aspects.

   In the longest independent episode in the book, Conrad's account of his experiences as a Carlist gunrunner
aboard the *Tremolino*,[27] the double focus created by Conrad's first-person narrative is especially important. Within
certain limits an exceptionally fine piece of writing, the
story of the *Tremolino* is precisely that, a *story:* no mere
anecdote, this narrative contains several fully developed
characters and a plot that moves toward a climax of high
interest and genuine finality. It is an unabashed adventure tale, starring Conrad as Errol Flynn. With three
other callow adventurers, Conrad forms a syndicate to
purchase the *Tremolino,* a very fast and very lovely sixty-
ton balancelle, for the purpose of smuggling weapons and
information into Spain in the cause of the royal pretender
Don Carlos. Under the joint command of Conrad and
Dominic Cervoni, a broad-chested, hairy Corsican with
"massive moustaches and . . . remorseless eyes," the *Tremolino* makes a number of successful voyages but is finally
betrayed by Dominic's nephew to the Spanish coastguard.
In the exciting sea-chase which follows, the *Tremolino*
loses half of her new mainsail, and in order to avoid capture Dominic and Conrad run the vessel onto a rock,
where she is destroyed and sunk. Then follows a Holly-
wood-perfect *dénouement* in which Dominic's traitorous

nephew, knocked overboard by his uncle, drowns in the rough seas because his body is heavily weighted with a money-belt full of gold he has stolen from Conrad's cabin, while Dominic himself, overcome by shame—"you may spit in Dominic's face because a traitor of our blood taints us all" (p. 182)—walks desolately away from the rock-strewn coast and out of Conrad's life forever.

Despite this furious action, the episode sustains for all of its nearly thirty pages the typically Conradian note which is sounded more briefly in "Initiation" and in the other anecdotal portions of *The Mirror of the Sea:* even in the episode's most dramatic moments, though somewhat more sparingly there than at other times, an amused tolerant irony marginally undercuts but never finally denies the glamor of innocent adventure. Here is Conrad describing the royalist syndicate of which he was a member: "If I mention that the oldest of us was very old, extremely old—nearly thirty years old—and that he used to declare with gallant carelessness, 'I live by my sword,' I think I have given enough information on the score of our collective wisdom" (p. 157). In the passages that immediately follow these lines, Conrad's summary of the character and ancestry of his fellows gestures toward the mock-heroic, recalling the catalogues of the hero's virtues and lineage which often precede Homeric battles. Such passages achieve an unambiguous deflation. But not all of the epical echoes in the *Tremolino* story are so simple. Something rather more subtle is at stake, for instance, when Conrad compares Dominic Cervoni to Odysseus:

> Astute and ruthless, he could have rivalled in resource the unfortunate son of Laertes and Anticlea. If he did not pit his craft and audacity against the very gods, it is only because the Olympian gods are dead. Certainly no woman could frighten him. A one-eyed giant would not have had the ghost of a chance against Dominic Cervoni, of Cor-

> sica, not Ithaca; and no king, son of kings, but of very re-
> spectable family—authentic Caporali, he affirmed. But
> that is as it may be. The Caporali families date back to
> the twelfth century. [p. 163]

The ironic pressures here, directed as much against the
adventure myth itself as against Dominic, are clear
enough, but so is the implication that Conrad's friend is
in some sense worthy, after all, of the comparison.

Throughout the *Tremolino* episode Conrad reminds us
of Dominic's near-epic stature, and such reminders serve
his art in several ways. First, as with his similar treatment
of men like Singleton, MacWhirr, Allistoun, and (in a different but related way) Kurtz, Conrad gives us a figure
who is larger than life and so in a sense deserves the extravagant action that is basic to his story. Second, by com-
paring Dominic to earlier adventurers of legend and of
history, he explains Dominic's great appeal to the romantic boy he had been, and, far more importantly, at the
same time brings to bear on his story that long tradition
of shared danger which, as I suggested above, can begin to
sanction his dependence on the material of the common
adventure tale:

> I [was] . . . fascinated by [Dominic's] . . . black hood
> turned immovably over the stern, as if in unlawful com-
> munion with that old sea of magicians, slave-dealers, ex-
> iles, and warriors, the sea of legends and terrors, where
> the mariners of remote antiquity used to hear the restless
> shade of an old wanderer weep aloud in the dark. [p.
> 176]

Finally, because such comparisons are highly literate explanations written after the fact, and because they slow
down the action in order to comment on it, they insist on
the presence of the older man who is telling the story, and
thus in some degree deflect our attention away from the

potential excesses of the plot and toward the narrator himself, whose complicated responses to his own story come to have an independent interest rivaling the adventure itself.

Though for the most part subordinated (but never obliterated) by the sheer action of the story, this secondary interest is the partial subject of the episode's great final paragraph, a paragraph in which Conrad returns to his identification of Dominic with Odysseus and in which the earlier irony has been absorbed by a high and unsentimental nostalgia. By beginning the quotation with the next-to-last paragraph, also wonderfully written with the exception of one weak sentence, it is possible to see how inevitably in the best Conrad specific events can generate larger significance:

> [Dominic] turned and walked away from me along the bank of the stream, flourishing a vengeful arm and repeating to himself slowly, with savage emphasis: "Ah! *Canaille Canaille! Canaille!* . . ." He left me there trembling with weakness and mute with awe. Unable to make a sound, I gazed after the strangely desolate figure of that seaman carrying an oar on his shoulder up a barren, rock-strewn ravine under the dreary leaden sky of *Tremolino*'s last day. Thus, walking deliberately, with his back to the sea, Dominic vanished from my sight.
>
> With the quality of our desires, thoughts, and wonder proportioned to our infinite littleness we measure even time itself by our own stature. Imprisoned in the house of personal illusions thirty centuries in mankind's history seem less to look back upon than thirty years of our own life. And Dominic Cervoni takes his place in my memory by the side of the legendary wanderer on the sea of marvels and terrors, by the side of the fatal and impious adventurer, to whom the evoked shade of the soothsayer predicted a journey inland with an oar on his shoulder, till he met men who had never set eyes on ships and oars. It

> seems to me I can see them side by side in the twilight of
> an arid land, the unfortunate possessors of the secret lore
> of the sea, bearing the emblem of their hard calling on
> their shoulders, surrounded by silent and curious men:
> even as I, too, having turned my back upon the sea, am
> bearing those few pages in the twilight, with the hope of
> finding in an inland valley the silent welcome of some pa-
> tient listener. [pp. 182–83; ellipsis Conrad's]

Nearly all the controlling themes of the *Tremolino* episode and of the entire book are compressed into these
lines. The flesh-and-blood Dominic, so vividly there,
walks out of Conrad's life but is fixed in memory, where
he is elevated to mythic significance and where he comes
to stand not only with the figures of legend but also with
those real men, like him captains and teachers to the
young Conrad, about whom we have been told earlier in
The Mirror of the Sea. And Dominic's friend, the youthful Conrad, standing alone near the sea in the dramatic
finale of the adventure that began his manhood, is juxtaposed against the older writer who in his final sentence di-
rects our attention to *his* adventure, which was the writing of the story. The complex relation between the
narrating voice and the matter of the story, a relation that
is focused in the final paragraph, redeems the episode's
conventional adventure elements, chastens the melodrama
of the plot, and frees Conrad's nostalgia from sentimentality. We feel especially that the nostalgia is hard and serious and worthy: in a word, that it has been earned.

The uses to which Conrad puts his first-person method
in the *Tremolino* episode are, as I shall show later,
deepened profoundly in the great fiction. But the relevant
point for the moment is simply that the techniques of this
semi-autobiographical fragment directly adumbrate the essential techniques of *Heart of Darkness, Lord Jim,* and
Under Western Eyes. Although in these works Conrad

more fully exploits the advantages of the self-conscious narrator, those advantages are also crucial in this finest chapter from *The Mirror of the Sea*.

It would be misleading, however, to end on this note, for the *Tremolino* episode remains an exciting adventure tale in which the action itself is paramount. It is a satisfying adventure, gracefully handled, its extravagance checked sufficiently to avoid the clichés and triviality potential in the worn convention from which it derives. The major interests of the piece are admirably simple, and it is probably true, as Leo Gurko has written, that in this episode, and in the whole of *The Mirror of the Sea,* "Conrad glorifies the very ideals, like fidelity, courage and craftsmanship, whose adequacy he challenges in his fiction." [28] Such a judgment, however, is less damaging than it may seem, since those values remain vital in Conrad even when they are severely challenged, and Conrad never surrenders his conviction of their necessity, however conscious he is of their limitations. Moreover, if we pay attention to what happens in the *Tremolino* episode, it becomes fairly clear that the ideals of loyalty and courage are not in the least easily triumphant. In the typically Conradian test of manliness that the young hero faces, his own resources fail him, and he regains his self-command only with the moral aid of a fellow sailor. Again, the action of the story turns on a betrayal and ends in a catastrophe which even Dominic, the embodiment of masculine courage and fidelity, a man entirely "initiated into the most awful mysteries of the sea" (p. 164), is powerless to avoid.[29] And finally, as I will show in the next chapter, in their lonely fraternity aboard the *Tremolino,* Conrad and Dominic are joined together in an imperiled partnership whose essential nature is celebrated repeatedly in Conrad's finest fiction.

4 Conrad's Romanticism

"I will sing a sweeter song tomorrow"

To acknowledge Conrad's dependence on the conventions
of the adventure story is to understand with particular
clarity how taxing must have been his struggle to avoid
the easy high rhetoric, the simplistic primitivism, the melodrama characteristic of a debased Romanticism. As I suggested earlier, this struggle was the more severe because
the nature of the personal experiences on which Conrad
drew for his stories and aspects at least of his own temperament combined to make him peculiarly susceptible to
the unjustified extravagance, the untruthfulness, that we
associate with popular exotic fiction. Indeed, the arc of his
career indicates that his struggle against these hazards was
intermittent and not consistently successful.

A novel like *Romance,* both because of what it adumbrates of Conrad's fine work and because of what it fails to
do, may be said, therefore, to have an importance in Conrad's *oeuvre* that far exceeds its aesthetic merit. For *Romance* is one of those books, like Stevenson and Lloyd
Osbourne's *The Wrecker* (1891), that attempts to mediate
between pure escapist adventure and "serious" fiction.
Like *The Wrecker, Romance* fails in this attempt. But we
can see in the very pretentiousness of its rhetoric a potential seriousness, an interest (however forced and unconvincing in this context) in the moral implications of its
hero's experiences. The book means to be taken seriously,
and its authors appear at least in some degree to have
done so. The following are Conrad's words:

> We try to produce a variation from the usual type of ro-
> mance our point of view being that the feeling of the ro-

mantic in life lies principally in the glamour memory
throws over the past and arises from the contact with a
different race and a different temperament; so that the
Spanish girl seems romantic to Kemp while that ordinary good young man seems romantic and even heroic
not only to Seraphina but to Sanchez and Don Riego
too.[1]

That these intentions are not realized in the novel is perhaps less important than that Conrad articulated them in
this excerpt from his letters. For it cannot be without significance that Conrad and Ford began to work together
on *Romance* as early as 1898 and that their writing of the
book continued, with interruptions, until sometime in
1902—the very period in which Conrad first succeeded
fully and subtly in transforming the conventions of adventure in works like *Heart of Darkness, Lord Jim, Typhoon,*
and *Nostromo.* It is not necessary to argue that intense
work on *Romance* preceded all these stories in order to
recognize that the collaboration presents us with a clear
partial instance of Conrad's involvement in the kinds of
problems with which he contended in these greater works.

Perhaps the chief reason for *Romance*'s failure to realize the serious intentions set forth in the letter quoted
above is the book's unconvincing narrative voice. The difference between that voice and Marlow's is striking and
most revealing. In *Romance* the first-person narrator
never earns the right to his frequent moral generalizations, and although we are told many times that this narrator is older than the young man who acts out the story,
there is no evidence that he is markedly different in out-
look, intelligence, or experience from the younger self
whose adventures he is recounting. Unlike Marlow, whose
anguish over the job of telling his story in *Lord Jim,* as in
Heart of Darkness, dramatizes his awareness of the integrity and pressing importance of the events he has endured

and waited many years to tell, the narrator of *Romance*
tells his story with a facile confidence that in the end implies a kind of contempt for the very experiences he has
been claiming are so profound and decisive. It is Marlow
whose self-conscious hesitations and evasive digressions
truly respect the primacy of experience; and it is Kemp in
Romance, like his counterparts in all conventional adventure stories, whose ease of telling implicitly repudiates the
claims his story appears to make for the unique and specially intense character of the adventurous life.

In this negative way, *Romance* proclaims the fullness
with which Conrad in his best books mastered the perils
that beset him. And insofar as he freed himself from the
triviality and mere appeal to novelty characteristic of the
popular exotic fiction of his day, Conrad was not so much
anticipating modern developments as returning to earlier,
more problematic and genuine versions of Romantic subject matter. As recent critics have made clear in the case of
Stevenson, the essential premises of the adventure story
originate in the defining pieties of the Romantic movement.[2] But in such stories, especially those written in the
eighties and nineties, they are debased pieties now, so reduced in intensity and seriousness as to constitute not the
visionary and *tentative* assertions of a Wordsworth, but
the simplistic assumptions of the middlebrow reading
public. It is one of Conrad's chief distinctions, though he
is rarely honored for it, to have written in this popular
mode and to have exploited precisely these tired and apparently exhausted pieties with a full conscious energy
that renews their vigor and rediscovers their high seriousness.

Conrad's characteristic and recurring story is a clearly
Romantic bildungsroman—"It is the Romantics," says
one of our best critics, "who first explored the dangerous
passageways of maturation" [3]—a bildungsroman cast

usually in the form of a voyage out into an uncluttered, elementary world that appears to promise self-discovery, growth, personal renewal. Conrad's protagonists leave the ordinary, the "civilized" world, or think they do, and travel to primitive regions where they are tested, if not by a nature alive with magical and demonic powers, at least by a nature whose menace and strangeness retain something of the old enchantment. A man is judged partly by his willingness to try himself in these exotic places, as the narrator in *Victory* indicates when he remarks that "men who went home" surrendered their adventurers' credentials and "did not count any more" (p. 23).

Set over against this fledgling voyager in the prototypal Conrad tale are two (usually) older figures. The first is the retainer character I have already discussed, a companion or mentor for the young hero. The second figure, also experienced where the young man is not, is the witness or observer, the teller of the story. Sometimes, as in "Youth" or *Heart of Darkness,* this teller is the young man grown older, looking back now in memory at the self he had been; elsewhere, as in *Lord Jim* or *Chance* or *Under Western Eyes,* this narrator describes not his own experiences but those of another. But in both versions the narrating voice is explicitly separated temporally and ontologically from the protagonist of the story, and this separation—which often determines both the shape and the meaning of Conrad's fiction—links the author of *Lord Jim* to the Romantic poets even more decisively than his fondness for exotic settings or his frequent reliance on variations of quest romance. It is striking, in fact, how closely Conrad's most characteristic works resemble what M. H. Abrams has identified as the greater Romantic lyric, a poetic form whose defining features are the play of memory across time and the juxtaposing of an older poet with his younger self.[4]

The central poems of the English Romantics and many
Conrad works focus especially on the extraordinary distance between narrator and actor, between the active,
unreflective young voyager in his glad animal vitality and
his older self, wiser perhaps, but also passive, somehow diminished. Conrad's speakers are often more ironic about
their younger incarnations, but Wordsworth is scarcely void
of such irony—the naive wanderer in "Resolution and In-
dependence" is one example. In any event, both writers
are heavy with nostalgia, and something more than nostalgia, over what the self must yield up to experience. And
in both there are clear intimations that this loss involves,
particularly, a rare quickness, a splendor or radical po-
tency of being.

The Conrad work that develops this notion most fully
—it is implicit nearly everywhere—is perhaps *Under
Western Eyes,* that Dostoyevskian political fable which
twists (but not quite beyond recognition) the usual Conradian adventure plot but which preserves and even extends the interior voyage of discovery that nearly always
in Conrad, as in the Romantic poets, parallels these outer
journeys. In *Under Western Eyes* the old teacher of lan-
guages who tells the story is, it is more than hinted, liter-
ally impotent, a kind of pathetic, unconscious rival for the
hand of Natalia Haldin. This narrator is a man whose passive skills as pedant and editor are meant to expose his
inadequacy as a reporter of the violent, driven lives of the
central characters. As the title suggests, the Western narrator confronts the seething energies of this Russian story as
an outsider, an alien, at once attracted and repelled by
what he calls the "terrible corroding simplicity" of the
characters in his story, yearners after apocalypse who
"detest"—these are his words—"the irremediable life of
the earth as it is" (p. 104). This narrator's profound am-

bivalence toward his story—his strained groveling confessions of impotence consorting uneasily with condescending assertions of his superiority—measures and exposes a
need he shares with nearly all Conradian narrators: a
need, which sometimes shades into outright obsession, to
thrust himself between the story and the reader, to deflect
attention away from the tale and toward the teller, as if in
this way to claim for himself, to absorb into himself, the
fierce living energies of the world he describes but cannot
fully enter.

Conrad's fondness for profoundly self-conscious and
self-dramatizing narrators is usually seen as a mark of his
modernity, as one of his clearest links with the self-absorption that characterizes so much twentieth-century fiction.
There seems no question of Conrad's influence in the
work of such novelists as Gide, Mann, and Faulkner, and
he seems an equally powerful presence for contemporary
writers like John Barth, Borges, Nabokov, and Doris Les-
sing. But what does seem questionable is the assumption
that the prominent self-consciousness of these writers is a
phenomenon that begins, essentially, in our own century.
Two things, especially, call this assumption into doubt.
There is, first, the disquieting fact that from the moment
of its birth, the novel as a form seems given to a radical,
mocking awareness of itself as artifice. *Don Quixote,* after
all, is the most self-conscious of books and is as obsessed as
Nabokov's *Pale Fire* with the precariousness of human fictions.

> In order to test [his helmet's] . . . strength and see if it
> was swordproof, [Quixote] . . . drew his sword and gave
> it two strokes, the first of which instantly destroyed the re-
> sult of a week's labor. It troubled him to see with what
> ease he had broken the helmet in pieces, so to protect it
> from such an accident, he remade it and fenced the inside

> with a few bars of iron in such a manner that he felt as-
> sured of its strength, and without caring to make a second
> trial, he held it to be a most excellent helmet.[5]

Ian Watt's account of the rise of the novel seems relevant here, for his description of the philosophic and social
pressures that lie back of the novel makes clear that the
genre's commitment to what he calls "formal realism" involves at least implicitly a nominalist attitude toward language, a concern with the distance between words and
real objects.[6] If Watt is right, then the novel as a genre—
its very existence as a literary kind dependent upon its
commitment to a particularizing, concretizing realism—
would appear to be caught from the very beginning in a
continual crisis of self-doubt and self-examination.
"Words, as is well known," says the narrator of *Under
Western Eyes,* "are the great foes of reality" (p. 3).

More important, if the existence of novels like *Don
Quixote* and *Tristram Shandy* casts doubt on the facile assumption that self-consciousness is the special mark of our
modern literature, there is also the fact that the old notion of a radical break or discontinuity between Romanticism and modernism has been shown to be largely
specious. In this respect as in others, criticism of fiction
has not kept pace with the scholarship that has grown out
of the study of poetry. In the work, especially, of
Geoffrey Hartman, Northrop Frye, Robert Langbaum,
M. H. Abrams, and Harold Bloom we are confronted
with varying and powerful evidence for an essential continuity between the Age of Wordsworth and ourselves—
and for a continuity based in part on a recognition of self-
consciousness as a specially Romantic malaise.[7]

An impulse deriving from this Romantic self-consciousness is expressed covertly in the conventional adventure

story, which tends to celebrate virtues that are typically
masculine and active. Dominic Cervoni, like his fellows
elsewhere in Conrad and still more like many characters
in Stevenson, Rider Haggard, Kipling, Marryat, Fenimore
Cooper, even Hemingway, is courageous, loyal, skilled in
his craft, and taciturn. His taciturnity is particularly emphasized. He speaks only when it is essential to the job at
hand and then with quiet succinctness.

This emphasis is entirely consonant with the traditional
expectations of the adventure mode which, because it is
focused on events, on action, almost inevitably comes to
value deeds over words, men of action over men of eloquence and contemplation. Because of its (often simplistic)
commitment to what are held to be the deeper and more
primitive human realities, the exotic adventure yarn, always by implication and in many cases explicitly, involves
a rejection of the civilized, the controlled, the "artificial."
Many of Stevenson's theoretical pronouncements about fiction are grounded in just such a rejection,[8] one consequence of which may be a bias not only against reflective
characters, but also against characters who are able to express themselves in more than monosyllables.

In Marryat's *Mr. Midshipman Easy* this typical inclination of the adventure story becomes a source of comedy.
The young hero, Jack Easy, has been ill-fitted for the maritime life, and indeed (so the novel suggests) for every
other sort of life, by a father who has trained him in philosophic disputation:

> Nothing pleased Mr. Easy so much as Jack's loquacity.
> "That's right; argue the point, Jack—argue the point,
> boy" would he say, as Jack disputed with his mother. And
> then he would turn to the Doctor, rubbing his hands, and
> observe, "Depend upon it, Jack will be a great, a very
> great man." [9]

Aboard ship, Jack will have his loquacity beaten out of him and will come to respect the example of taciturn, almost inarticulate competence set for him by his superior officers and especially by Mesty, the African savage turned sailor who becomes his partner and moral guide early in the novel and sticks by his side thereafter, the very type of the faithful retainer.

What Marryat's unpretentious and often charming boy's story uses for comedy, other adventure stories—by Rider Haggard, Stevenson, Kipling especially—use with unsmiling solemnity. And something of the same bias against characters who are reflective or verbal survives powerfully in Conrad, although with even the simplest of Conrad's sailors, as with Wordsworth's rustics, one senses what Marlow says of Lord Jim: "He was not eloquent, but there was a dignity in this constitutional reticence, there was a high seriousness in his stammerings" (p. 248).

Conrad's boldest if least nuanced treatment of this theme is *The Nigger of the "Narcissus,"* where inarticulateness is the very mark of seamanly virtue and where, conversely, to be talkative is to reveal one's unmanly wickedness. The novel dramatizes this idea most fully in the opposition of Singleton and Donkin. The former lives among the crew "taciturn and unsmiling" (p. 41), his silence and simplicity the very source of his heroism. Symbolically named, Singleton belongs to a dying species of "voiceless men," a generation "inarticulate and indispensable," whose modern successors are no longer "strong and mute" because "if they have learned how to speak they have also learned how to whine" (p. 25). Donkin embodies this new generation of whining complainers; he is a bad sailor, a conniving malingerer, and so a "consummate artist" (p. 100) whose "picturesque and filthy loquacity flowed like a troubled stream from a poisoned source" (p. 101). These matters are distilled for us early in the novel when Donkin makes his first appearance in the forecastle: "A taciturn long-armed shellback, with hooked fingers, who had been lying on his back smoking, turned in his bed to examine him dispassionately, then, over his head, sent a long jet of saliva towards the door" (p. 10).

When Conrad defines Donkin's contemptible essence by calling him a consummate artist he is expressing with extraordinary directness the antiliterary side of his nature that is disclosed also in his letters and autobiographical writing. There is in Conrad a deep division, a radical conflict, between the seaman's vocation and the artist's. It is a conflict that is undisguised and recurrent in his correspondence, and however much unease it may have caused Conrad the man, it was also a conflict that enlarged and enriched his fiction.

In his letters Conrad may be said to vacillate between moments of almost religious commitment to the act of writing and other moments of deep disdain for the passive, inactive life of the artist. He could in certain moods attain to the exalted tone of the preface to *The Nigger of the "Narcissus,"* as in this sentence from a letter to E. V. Lucas: "A man who puts forth the secret of his imagination to the world accomplishes, as it were, a religious rite." [10] But he could, on the other hand, lament his kinship with literary men and align himself with mariners like old Singleton or even MacWhirr:

> I've never had the pleasure of meeting [Admiral Sir William Robert Kennedy (1838–1916)] . . . ; but I've read and admired his book [*Hurrah for the Life of a Sailor: Fifty Years in the Navy* (1901)]. Now a book of that sort *is* the man—the man disclosed absolutely; and the contact of such a genuine personality is like an invigorating bath for one's mind jaded by infinite effort after literary expression, wearied by all the unrealities of a writing life, discouraged by a sunless, starless sort of men-

tal solitude, having lost its reckoning in a grey sea of
words, words, words; an unruly choppy sea running cross-
wise in all the endless shifts of thought. Oh! for a cutter
and the Fatshan Creek, or for that wonderful beat-up
from Mozambique Channel to Zanzibar! A wrestle with
wind and weather has a moral value like the primitive
acts of faith on which may be built a doctrine of salvation and a rule of life. At any rate men engaged in such
contests have been my spiritual fathers too long for me
to change my convictions—if I have pulled off my sea-
boots, hung the sou'wester on a peg and made a tasteful
trophy of my pet marline spikes.[11]

It is unarguably true that Conrad's fiction dramatizes—
sometimes with great ambiguity but often quite openly as
well—his conviction that such captains and men of action
are his spiritual fathers. In a revealing passage from *The
Mirror of the Sea* he presses this notion still further,
claiming that his sense of vocation as an artist has been
shaped by the example of such master mariners:

> Some of the masters whose influence left a trace upon my
> character to this very day, combined a fierceness of concep-
> tion with a certitude of execution upon the basis of just
> appreciation of means and ends which is the highest qual-
> ity of the man of action. And an artist is a man of action,
> whether he creates a personality, invents an expedient, or
> finds the issue of a complicated situation. [p. 33]

One can, I suppose, understand something of what Conrad means when he asserts that the artist is a man of action. But it is difficult not to perceive in that assertion
more private necessity than objective truth. One of Conrad's earliest critics, referring to this same passage from
The Mirror of the Sea, saw the essential point: "This
strange confusion of species, this perhaps wilful blurring
of radical distinctions between the dreaming and the prac-

tical mind, is explicable only by Conrad's need to see himself as a man of action, in touch with life." [12]

Some such need surely lies behind Conrad's pressing distrust of his art. It is a need that is generated in part by Conrad's sometimes desperate awareness of his own limitations:

> To be able to think and unable to express is a fine torture. I am undergoing it—without patience. I don't see the end of it. . . . Now I've got all my people together I don't know what to do with them. The progressive episodes of the story *will* not emerge from the chaos of my sensations. I feel nothing clearly. And I am frightened when I remember that I have to drag it all out of myself.

> I am trying to write the *Rescue* and all my ambition is to make it good enough for a magazine—readable in a word. I doubt whether I can. I struggle without pleasure like a man certain of defeat.[13]

From one perspective, these moments of almost neurotically intense self-criticism may be said to imply Conrad's high artistic standards, his respect for the seriousness and value of literature. But from another angle, such exclamations of despair may be said to express his acute sense of the elusive integrity of experience itself. The excessive self-calumnies that run through the correspondence are in part a consequence not only of Conrad's frustration with his own talent but also of his abiding preoccupation with the gulf between art and life.

That preoccupation pressed upon Conrad the potentially disabling suspicion that the complexities of life lie beyond the reach of language. Both in his letters and in the fiction itself, Conrad seems frequently to doubt with all the corrosive desperation of his skeptical temperament the usefulness of *any* word, and he often expresses the fear that the enterprise of literature is an impossible delusion.

> Half the words we use have no meaning whatever and of
> the other half each man understands each word after the
> fashion of his own folly and conceit.[14]

> If I have ever had these gifts [of imagination and expres-
> sion] in any sort of living form they have been smothered
> out of existence a long time ago under a wilderness of
> words. Words, as is well known, are the great foes of real-
> ity. [*Under Western Eyes*, p. 3]

This doubt about the usefulness of language is not for
Conrad merely an easy commonplace or an unexamined
assumption. It is a tested if melancholy aesthetic principle, a recognition of limitation and even of failure that is
the more weighty because it has been consciously acknowledged. Though this principle is dramatized richly and
fully in the fiction, its force rarely becomes explicit in the
letters because Conrad was apparently reluctant to discuss
his own work in serious detail and preferred not to subject the work of his friends to rigorous analysis. But in
one revealing letter to Hugh Clifford, Conrad does provide a statement of his convictions about the limits of language, and this letter is as important as the preface to *The
Nigger of the "Narcissus"* for an understanding of Conrad's fundamentally Romantic vision of the burdens and
possibilities of art. The letter is a critique of Clifford's
memoir, *In a Corner of Asia* (1899), which Conrad ad-
mired but felt to be poorly written. He begins his criticism by suggesting that minute attention to phrasing is a
necessity, that art is rigorous and careful:

> Words, groups of words, words standing alone, are sym-
> bols of life, have the power in their sound or their aspect
> to present the very thing you wish to hold up before the
> mental vision of your readers. The things "as they are"
> exist in words; therefore words should be handled with
> care lest the picture, the image of truth abiding in facts,
> should become distorted—or blurred.

These are the considerations for a mere craftsman—you may say; and you may also conceivably say that I have nothing else to trouble my head about. However, the *whole* of the truth lies in the presentation; therefore, the expression should be studied in the interest of veracity. This is the only morality of *art* apart from *subject*.

But as he proceeds to illustrate his specific objections to Clifford's prose, it becomes clear that art is also humble. He begins his close analysis by quoting one of Clifford's sentences:

"When the whole horror of his position forced itself with an agony of realization upon his frightened mind, Pa' Tûa for a space lost his reason." . . . In this sentence the reader is borne down by the full expression. The words: *with an agony of realization* completely destroy the effect—therefore interfere with the truth of the statement. The word *frightened* is fatal. It seems as if it had been written without any thought at all. It takes away all sense of reality—for if you read the sentence *in its place on the page* you will see that the word *"frightened"* (or indeed any word of the sort) is inadequate to express the true state of that man's mind. No word is adequate.[15]

No word is adequate. There are aspects of experience that lie beyond the reach of language, and it is the obligation of the serious writer to confront and act upon these limitations.

Conrad is the victim, then, as were the Romantic poets before him, of profound and wholly conscious uncertainties about the reaches of art. Both a sailor and a writer about sailors, Conrad is an artist whose respect for literature is exceeded by his respect for experience. And because these preoccupations feed into and trouble his fiction, Conrad's major works are set decisively apart from stories of conventional adventure, whose latent hostility to the verbal and the artful is never consciously acknowledged or understood.

We can see the barest shadow of those preoccupations
in Conrad's repeated juxtapositions of talkers and doers,
in the oppositions he establishes between men of pragmatic simplicity and men of cunning and seductive eloquence. Thus, as I noted above, Donkin is played off
against Singleton in *The Nigger of the "Narcissus."* And
there are particularly rich instances of such oppositions in
Lord Jim, for example, where the shrill eloquence of Cor-
nelius and the vivid rantings of Gentleman Brown contrast
with the actions of taciturn men like the French Lieuten-
ant and Captain Brierly. *Typhoon* gives us a semicomic
version of a similar opposition, for in that story Mac-
Whirr's ambiguous fraternity with his first-mate Jukes is
an alliance of unimaginative, even stupid competence with
self-conscious and quavering intellection; an alliance between a captain "who found very little occasion to talk"
(p. 90) and his loquacious first officer; an alliance, appropriately, between a man who writes brief, dull letters and
a man whose letters, however self-involved, are thoughtful
and interesting. Again, in *Under Western Eyes* Conrad relies in a fundamental way on our distaste for certain kinds
of eloquence. The reader's harsh judgment of Peter Ivanovitch, for example, is a consequence not primarily of his involvement in revolutionary activities but of the fact that
he cheapened his heroic escape from Russia *by writing
about it,* by trading in words upon his exploits. Similarly,
Sophia Antonovna seems to Razumov more appealing
than Ivanovitch because, despite her fanaticism, she is
"stripped of rhetoric, mysticism and theories" (p. 261).
And Razumov himself, "a comparatively taciturn personality" (p. 6), "a man of few words" (p. 173), "a silent man"
(p. 255), appears least sympathetic during his return from
Ziemianitch's stable when, walking in the Moscow streets,
he compromises his essential nature by growing eloquent
in betrayal, "holding a discourse with himself with ex-

traordinary abundance and facility" (p. 35). In such discourse Razumov justifies his decision to betray Haldin,
and the glibness of his rationalization is offensive. Later
in the novel, when the reader's sympathy has shifted almost wholly toward Razumov, one finds that his essential
trait is again taciturnity; confronted by the furious and
absurd eloquence of Ivanovitch and the imperceptive
wordiness of the English narrator, Razumov's mute suffering is more appealing than any rhetoric.

One could multiply these examples and consider each
more fully; but I will end with the reminder that Donkin's most striking counterpart in Conrad's work, even
more clearly a "consummate artist," is Kurtz in *Heart of
Darkness,* who (we learn) is both a painter and a poet and
whose distinguishing characteristic is his "magnificent eloquence." The deep ambiguity in Conrad's attitude to language as a means of illumination and insight but also as a
source of delusion and treachery is focused in Kurtz—and
in Marlow, himself an eloquent man, whose mingling of
admiration and disdain and even terror at Kurtz's example is a dramatic reflection of Conrad's own ambivalence.

The remarkable directness of Conrad's disapproval of
Donkin's writerly loquacity and, still more, his open and
fully acknowledged ambivalence concerning Kurtz's dark
eloquence, as I have already suggested, help to distinguish
him from writers like Kipling, Marryat, the early Stevenson. The books of these men implicitly attack artifice, intellection, language, without ever accepting full responsibility for such an attack; while in Conrad, as in the
Romantic poets, the man's suspicion of art and of language, of the hesitations and limits of intellect, is translated into the artist's conscious subject matter.

We begin to close with that subject matter—with Conrad's abiding Romantic preoccupation with the reaches
and limits of language—in the character of Lord Jim, af-

flicted at the inquiry into his desertion by his acute sense
of the inviolable integrity of any single moment of experience, undone (finally) by his discovery that the very pulse
and intensity of experience passes away in the instant of
its occurring:

> He wanted to go on talking for truth's sake, perhaps for
> his own sake also; and while his utterance was deliberate,
> his mind positively flew round and round the serried cir-
> cle of facts that had surged up all about him to cut him
> off from the rest of his kind: it was like a creature that,
> finding itself imprisoned within an enclosure of high
> stakes, dashes round and round, distracted in the night,
> trying to find a weak spot, a crevice, a place to scale.
> [p. 31]

This compelling vision of a man caught in the imprisoning privacy of his own experiences defines one of Conrad's deepest fears, enacts one of this novel's crucial insights and, finally, begins to explain the fevered erratic
shifting of the book's narrative form. Again and again in
Lord Jim both Marlow and Jim himself will be caught in
similar circumstances. Repeatedly, we see Jim gesturing
with at best feeble success toward communication with
other men. Just as he fails to explain himself at the inquiry, so he fails again in his long communing with Marlow at dinner after the first day of the hearing. Similarly,
in his final interview with Jewel he discovers that he cannot explain why he must desert her. Again, in the final
crisis on Patusan, Jim turns writer for a brief instant, once
more undone by the recalcitrant privacy of the reality he
lives but cannot fathom or describe:

> It is . . . impossible to say whom he had in his mind
> when he seized the pen: Stein—myself—the world at
> large—or was this only the aimless startled cry of a soli-
> tary man confronted by his fate? "An awful thing has
> happened," he wrote before he flung the pen down for

the first time; look at the ink blot resembling the head of an arrow under these words. After a while he had tried again, scrawling heavily, as if with a hand of lead, another line. "I must now at once . . ." The pen had spluttered, and that time he gave it up. There's nothing more; he had seen a broad gulf that neither eye nor voice could span. I can understand this. He was overwhelmed by the inexplicable. [pp. 340–41; first ellipsis mine]

Marlow, too, like many Conrad characters and especially narrators, `is overwhelmed, or nearly so, by the inexplicable. And the description of Jim trapped in an enclosure of the self and scrabbling in fevered bafflement to escape is also the very image of Marlow's condition. In *Lord Jim,* as elsewhere, the Conrad narrator's confessions of failure are so frequent they resemble a refrain:

> All this happened in much less time than it takes to tell, since I am trying to interpret for you into slow speech the instantaneous effect of visual impressions. [p. 48]

> I can't explain to you who haven't seen him and who hear his words only at second hand. [p. 93]

> The blight of futility that lies in wait for men's speeches had fallen upon our conversation, and made it a thing of empty sounds. [p. 148]

> That was all then—and there shall be nothing more; there shall be no message, unless such as each of us can interpret for himself from the language of facts, that are so often more enigmatic than the craftiest arrangement of words. [p. 340]

Marlow's characteristic diction, his persistent reliance on what might be called a vocabulary of uncertainty, is intimately related to these confessions of limitation and bafflement. In *Lord Jim,* as in *Heart of Darkness,* the famous adjectival insistence which has so disturbed Leavis and others is for the most part an essential aspect of the novel's meaning.[16] For Marlow's fondness for vague, abstract adjectives—one might call them Shelleyan adjectives —reinforces his stated conviction that his telling must fall short of perfect truth. The drama of Marlow's rhetoric is a drama of Romantic aspiration and failure, a drama in which vividly precise scenic details are juxtaposed against an abstract commentary which continually calls that scenic vividness into question or which insists on its radical incompleteness. "I cannot paint/What then I was," cries Wordsworth in *Tintern Abbey,* though he tries in the very next phrase, resorting to a metaphor whose tentative, problematic quality is especially clear because it follows upon this confession of limitation and failure. "The sounding cataract/Haunted me like a passion." Marlow's eloquence, like Wordsworth's, is driven, tentative, self-doubting: a harsh, earned eloquence which registers, above all, a fundamental humility.

Something of that humility, though a touch of artist's pride as well, is present, too, in Marlow's explicit awareness of the fact that there is a sense in which Jim's very existence depends upon his skill as a narrator.

> I am telling you so much about my own instinctive feelings and bemused reflections because there remains so little to be told of him. He existed for me, and after all it is only through me that he exists for you. I've led him out by the hand; I have paraded him before you. [p. 224]

> This was, indeed, one of the lost, forgotten, unknown places of the earth; I had looked under its obscure surface; and I had felt that when to-morrow I had left it for ever, it would slip out of existence . . . I have that feeling about me now; perhaps it is that feeling which had incited me to tell you the story, to try to hand over to you, as it were, its very existence, its reality. [p. 323]

In these representative passages, as in Wordsworth's most characteristic lyrics, the reader is required to bear in mind simultaneously two distinct moments of time: first, the moment of the experience itself; and second, the *now* of Marlow's telling about that experience. Repeatedly throughout the novel, and in many other stories and novels, Conrad maintains, insists upon, this double perspective; repeatedly, as we hear about Jim we are forced also to attend to another and essentially separate story, the story of Marlow's attempt to communicate. Virtually all the impressionist strategies to which Marlow has recourse during his narrative—the jumbled, digressive chronology; the breaks in the story when Marlow interrupts himself to address his listeners or merely to pause reflectively; his persistent admissions of inadequacy; the adjectival diction —all these strategies serve not simply to show us, in the words of one of the novel's admirers, "how hard it is to know, and how hard to judge; and how hard even to separate the two processes." [17] They serve also to transform Marlow from a mere narrative convenience to a credibly evoked human being whose hesitations and failures and desperate involvement in the task of understanding and narrating constitute *in themselves* a compelling drama, a drama which rivals the more traditional story of Jim's adventures.

Marlow explicitly acknowledges the existence of this second story when he says that he finds himself caught in his "own instinctive and bemused reflections"—caught, that is, not in Jim's anguished career of failure, but in his own parallel anguish in this drama of the telling. And surely it is clear that in *Lord Jim,* as elsewhere, Marlow's credentials as a "teller" are far more impressive than his claims to seamanship. Though the reader is told about Marlow's vast experience as a captain, the Marlow whom the reader sees, the Marlow dramatized and brought to life in the novel, is no such man of action. He is, rather, the curious spectator who goes to the courtroom passively to observe the drama of another; he is the moralizing after-dinner talker, the letter-writing reporter. Paradoxically, we come to believe in Marlow the master mariner, the man committed to ideals of conduct that are defined by the seafaring tradition, only in the degree to which the desperation of his telling convinces us of the profoundly intimate way in which Jim's failure to honor the sailors' code threatens Marlow's sense of self. That is to say, we can accept Marlow's identity as a sea captain only because the novel insists so forcefully and so intensely upon his reality as a narrator.

First-person narrators, ostensibly like Marlow, are very common in the adventure mode, so common, indeed, that Henry James seems to have assumed that only in romance was such a narrative technique acceptable. Though condescending and perhaps arbitrary, James's distrust of the first person is of particular interest for students of Conrad. In a letter to Wells concerning the latter's *New Machiavelli,* James objected strongly to

> the bad service you have done your cause by riding so hard again that acurst autobiographic form which puts a premium on the loose, the improvised, the cheap and the easy. Save in the fantastic and the romantic (Copperfield, Jane Eyre, that charming thing of Stevenson's with the bad title—"Kidnapped"?) it has no authority, no persuasive or convincing force—its grasp of reality and truth isn't strong and disinterested.

He restates these objections in the preface to *The Ambassadors,* when he calls the first-person method "the darkest abyss of romance," a strategy "foredoomed to looseness"

and committed to "the terrible *fluidity* of self-revela-
tion." [18]

These remarks point to dangers that Conrad, in books
like *Lord Jim, Heart of Darkness,* and *Under Western
Eyes,* transforms into distinctive virtues. What Conrad has
clearly done in these works, as less intensively though still
effectively elsewhere, is to discover in the "acurst autobio-
graphic" quicksands of which James is so distrustful one
of his richest and most ambitious subjects. In Conrad's
hands, that is to say, the typical first-person narrator of the
conventional adventure story undergoes a radical transformation, his defining self-absorption deflecting attention
away from the potential extravagance implicit in the mere
facts of the story and toward that other drama which is enacted in his own anguish over the job of telling and understanding. That something resembling this kind of self-
consciousness is a common, even a wearying, feature of
contemporary fiction must not be held against Conrad,
who is the first novelist in English after Sterne to dramatize in all its complex seriousness his sense of limitation,
his recognition that there are many things words cannot
be expected to do. Like *Tristram Shandy,* but with a
more austere melancholy, *Lord Jim* is a novel about itself:
its (partial) subject is the drama which created it.

So, even more directly, is *Heart of Darkness.* As in *Lord
Jim,* the Marlow of the shorter work is obsessed with the
problem of using "mere words" to get at the "unspeak-
able" truths which his experiences in Africa have suggested to him. The abstract diction, the waywardly eccen-
tric narrative line, the interruptions and confessions of
failure—all are as central to *Heart of Darkness* as to *Lord
Jim.* If anything, these strategies are of greater importance
in the novella, because there Marlow himself is both actor
and narrator. In *Lord Jim* Conrad seems to maintain a

kind of balance between Jim's story and the story of Marlow's telling; but these proportions are shifted in *Heart of
Darkness*. Guerard and others are surely correct in their
claim that the novella is fundamentally Marlow's story: a
journey into regions where Marlow confronts, as in a
dream, aspects of himself.

Kurtz, the inner Marlow, the secret sharer, is variously
described: he is "magnificent" and "gifted," a sometime
member of "the gang of virtue." But the adjective applied
to Kurtz most often is "eloquent." As the steamer pene-
trates into the wilderness toward the inner station and the
"enchanted castle" of truth that Kurtz's presence there
embodies, Marlow hears of the turmoil downriver and is
appalled by the thought that Kurtz may be dead:

> I couldn't have been more disgusted if I had travelled
> all this way for the sole purpose of talking with Mr.
> Kurtz. Talking with . . . I . . . became aware that that
> was exactly what I had been looking forward to—a talk
> with Kurtz. I made the strange discovery that I had never
> imagined him as doing, you know, but as discoursing.
> . . . The man presented himself as a voice. Not of course
> that I did not connect him with some sort of action.
> Hadn't I been told . . . he had collected, bartered, swin-
> dled, or stolen more ivory than all the other agents to-
> gether? That was not the point. The point was in his
> being a gifted creature, and that of all his gifts the one
> that stood out preeminently, that carried with it a sense
> of real presence, was his ability to talk, his words—the
> gift of expression, the bewildering, the illuminating, the
> most exalted and the most contemptible, the pulsating
> stream of light, or the deceitful flow from the heart of an
> impenetrable darkness. [pp. 113–14; first ellipsis Con-
> rad's]

It is highly significant that the grandiloquent final sentence of this passage should respond with such extreme

ambivalence to the fact of Kurtz's eloquence: language *is* to Marlow, as to Conrad, at once bewildering and illuminating, and it is appropriate that Conrad's most ambiguous character, both villain and hero, should be a master of language. Though I have no wish to turn *Heart of Darkness* into a formal allegory, it seems impossible not to recognize in Marlow's mingled admiration and disdain for Kurtz something of Conrad's deep ambivalence toward the profession of the artist.

But it would be wrong to grant too much to Kurtz. The emphasis on craft and discipline in Marlow's account of his struggle to rebuild his steamer and then to navigate that narrowing dark river strengthens and complicates the art-theme, directing it toward Marlow himself. Conrad's doppelgängers have in general been granted more substance by modern readers than their spectral appearance or the actual proportions of the stories would seem to justify. Marlow and the narrator-captain of "The Secret Sharer" are the protagonists, Kurtz and Leggatt their shadows, cautionary partial-selves whose energies are acknowledged but also resisted. That *Heart of Darkness* is Marlow's story is always clear in the obsessive self-reflexiveness that declares itself so aggressively in nearly every paragraph and that forms and de-forms the richly idiosyncratic pattern of the novella as a whole. "No influential friend would have served me better," Marlow says of his vessel. "She had given me a chance to come out a bit—to find out what I could do" (p. 85). We might say the same of Marlow's experiences in his other, later adventure: the adventure of his telling.[19]

That adventure, it is clear, is more perilous, its success more limited and more ambiguous, than the African journey that is its source and cause. Even more extensively than in *Lord Jim,* Conrad here engages his deepest uncertainties about the enterprise of understanding and communication that is art. European culture's "civilizing" mission in the dark places of the earth is mocked and exposed by the story's radical pessimism, of course; and so are the various professions, the human vocations and purposes, which that culture tends especially to honor— explorer, sailor, politician, lawyer, director of companies. More penetrating and unsettling still, as Kurtz's eloquence and Marlow's tormented narrative indicate, art itself and even the grounds of Western epistemology are challenged by the darkness. The obstacles to knowing and recreating the world are personal and intimate in part: memory or sight may be faulty, confined by temperament and the limits of one's gifts. But they are also general or universal: what happened or what is will never fully yield to language and the ordering faculties of the mind.

Failure thus becomes Conrad's truest subject, and repeatedly in his best books the failures dramatized in the literal story are mirrored again in the falterings and confessions of inadequacy that rush from the mouths of his narrators. Marlow's lie to Kurtz's Intended (for but one example) is a confession of humanity and limitation that is enacted again in the painful, self-conscious hesitancy of Marlow the narrator's attempt to tell his story.

In the degree to which they exploit the advantages of the self-conscious narrator, *Heart of Darkness* and *Lord Jim* are unparalleled elsewhere in Conrad, although the narrator of *Under Western Eyes* resembles Marlow in essential respects and although in its own way *Nostromo* asserts even more fully than these three works its freedom from a consecutive chronology. But Conrad's consciousness of the disparity between deeds and words, between action and contemplation, deeply affects nearly all of his successful stories. For in virtually all the good fiction the carefully established poise between the past of the experience and the present of its telling remains a crucial strategy. In my discussion of the *Tremolino* episode from *The Mirror of the Sea* I tried to indicate how Conrad's affectionately ironic tone enforces an awareness of the vast differences between the young man experiencing the adventures and the older man who is telling about them. I suggested that this dual perspective, though far less insistent than the same thing in *Heart of Darkness,* carries the burden of rescuing Conrad's nostalgia from sentimentality and of renewing the largely conventional adventure plot. The same could be said of both "The Secret Sharer" and *The Shadow-Line*. In both stories, though with nothing like the obsessive fullness of his similar strategy in *Lord Jim,* Conrad takes care to remind us that the actor and the narrator of the story are not exactly the same person; he establishes a tone that calls our attention to the fact that the narrator has already lived through the experience he is describing and possesses therefore a maturity which distinguishes him from the younger self who is the subject of his narrative. However much *The Shadow-Line* and *Heart of Darkness* differ in tone, both stories show us a Conrad whose attention to matters of technique has been exceedingly rigorous. And it may be that the extreme self-consciousness of *Lord Jim,* or *Heart of Darkness,* or *Under Western Eyes* is meant to compensate for the greater extravagance, the clearer pull toward melodrama, in the essential material of these fictions. *The Shadow-Line,* after all, like "The Secret Sharer," is a spare story, less romantically plotted than the rest of Conrad, and so does not require flamboyant narrative strategies. What seems in any case beyond doubt is that when Conrad fails most disastrously, as in novels like *The Rover* or *The Rescue,* he does so not because he has stumbled into alien material—in bare outline *Lord Jim, Under Western Eyes,* and *Nostromo* are quite as melodramatic as any of the later books. Rather, he fails because he appears to have surrendered

the technical vigilance which characterizes his enduring
achievements, a vigilance revealed most decisively in the
anguished self-consciousness of his narrators.

Auden's elegy for Yeats addresses such anguished tellers: "Sing of human unsuccess/In a rapture of distress."
And a line from Faulkner, Conrad's greatest successor in
the uses of this drama of the telling, is relevant, too. This
is the line in *Absalom, Absalom!* in which General Comp-
son, Quentin's grandfather, defines language as "that meager and fragile thread by which the little surface corners
and edges of men's secret and solitary lives may be joined
for an instant now and then before sinking back into the
darkness." [20] Faulkner expresses here a very Conradian
and Romantic faith in language, in art, as an agency of
community, as a fragile but genuine counterforce to the
secrecy and solitariness of the human circumstance. And
this faith, however embattled, may distinguish the Romantic self-consciousness from the modern or the contemporary. This distinction, surely, is one of degree, not of
kind, but it seems to me significant, if only because it
joins Conrad's characteristic awareness of the gap between
language and reality to the Romantic agony rather than to
its contemporary versions.

Consider this great, bitter poem by J. V. Cunningham:

> Time will assuage.
> Time's verses bury
> Margin and page
> In commentary,
>
> For gloss demands
> A gloss annexed
> Till busy hands
> Blot out the text,
>
> And all's coherent.
> Search in this gloss

> No text inherent:
> The text was loss.
>
> The gain is gloss.[21]

The final pun is brilliant and terrifying: the gain is gloss
—it is dazzling, remarkable; but it is all gloss, it is *mere*
gloss, it includes nothing of the thing itself. Cunningham's resentment is contained by the terrible concision of
the dimeter line, by the enclosing rhymes, by the icy finality of his concluding pun. He is not desperate but coldly
imprisoned. There is space here for bitterness and for
tough, angry wit. But to struggle would be pointless. Cunningham's attitude is perhaps mirrored in the weary half-
silences of Beckett or in the mad ingenious puzzles of
Nabokov. But Conrad, like the English Romantic poets,
holds to a meager but partly sustaining faith in the power
of language to make sense of the world and, however imperfectly, to recreate it. "I cannot paint/What then I
was." But I will try and I will come close. Conrad's narrators, like Conrad himself, are perpetually dissatisfied,
obsessed by failure, driven repeatedly to renew their struggle, to tell the story in a new way or to investigate the facts
yet one more time. Their emblem might be the moving
and characteristically Romantic conclusion to Coleridge's
brief preface to *Kubla Khan,* in which the poet tells us
that he wrote the fragment which survives immediately
on waking from an opium dream and that an interruption
by "a person on business from Porlock" kept him from com-
pleting it. "The author has frequently purposed to
finish" the poem, Coleridge says, and quotes a line from
Theocritus which he has adapted for his purpose and
which translates as: "I will sing a sweeter song tomorrow."
To this Coleridge adds a mordant line of his own: "But
the tomorrow is yet to come."

PARTNERS AND ANCESTORS

"Things far distant, men who have lived"

Faulkner's menaced but surviving faith in the word as a fragile thread which may in some degree join men together, deny their separateness, implies that a sense of Other may help to rescue the Romantic desperation about language from total absorption or dissolution in the Self. The agony of the Conrad narrator is two-edged: like the speaker in a number of English Romantic poems, this narrator is constantly being drawn inward and through time toward the world of his reminiscence and also outward toward his auditors or readers. He is not, that is, characteristically engaged simply in the act of recreating or rediscovering for himself that younger self or past time which is the object of his remembering; he is also, and crucially, engaged in the equally difficult task of bringing that world and that younger self into contact with those who read or listen to him. "It is certain," said Novalis in a passage so important to Conrad that he used it as the epigraph to *Lord Jim* and again in a crucial moment in one of his autobiographical books,[22] "It is certain my conviction gains infinitely the moment another soul will believe in it."

All narrators are surrogates for the artist, and all are engaged in an act which mediates between the tale and its intended audience. But in Conrad and in the Romantic poems that most closely resemble his fiction this mediating role has a special urgency. The gesture of community implicit in any teller's decision to relate a story is acknowledged and lifted to particular prominence by Conrad's drama of the telling, by his insistent habit of setting the scene in which the telling occurs, of dwelling on the narrator's perplexities as well as on the protagonist's, of introducing auditors who converse with the narrator and even (as in *Lord Jim*) receive letters from him.

These and similar strategies have their counterpart in
Wordsworth's habit of addressing particular speakers—his
sister Dorothy and Coleridge especially—in a number of
his poems. The whole of the *Prelude* is addressed to Coleridge, and it is crucial to the poem's meaning that at key
moments Wordsworth speaks directly to him, reaching
out, one feels, for a friend's consoling and encouraging
sympathy. Coleridge, too, has some important poems—
including *To William Wordsworth* and the *Dejection
Ode*—in which the speaker implicates a particularized
auditor in the spiritual anguish he is evoking. These, as in
Conrad, are clearly gestures of inclusion and sharing—
very often punctuated by exclamation points to emphasize
the fervor and sincerity of the speaker's need for spiritual
company. They are gestures designed to create an alliance
of shared feeling that will bind the speaker and his sense
of what is important and humanly true to the validating
sympathies of another person. The conclusion of *Tintern
Abbey,* in which Wordsworth turns finally to the figure of
his sister for whatever consolation he can tentatively find
in her human presence and in her resemblance to his
younger self, is a specially clear and resonant example of
this crucial Romantic and Conradian procedure.

Wordsworth's sister serves in the poem as an assurance
of continuity—the continuity not simply of blood but of
those glad animal movements that Wordsworth had experienced in youth and inevitably lost but whose reappearance in his sister gives proof that human beings resemble
one another and share essential qualities. Conrad, too, I
have suggested earlier, is deeply preoccupied by the continuities between young and old, his most characteristic
situation being a kind of partnership—a meeting or join-
ing together of two characters, one young and inexperienced, the other usually older, whose role is that of guide
or teacher. The relationship between Dominic Cervoni
and the autobiographical Conrad in *The Mirror of the*

Sea provides a simplified version of this recurring Conradian alliance. Aboard the *Tremolino,* for example, pursued by their enemies, Conrad and Dominic discover that their ship has been sabotaged by one of the crew. "The experience of treachery" overwhelms the young Conrad, and "on the verge of tears" he finally stammers out his fear of capture (pp. 175, 176). It is the older, more experienced Dominic who reassures him and gives him back his courage, as MacWhirr's stolid presence saves Jukes in *Typhoon,* and as Ransome's calm certainty forces the new captain in *The Shadow-Line* to accept the responsibilities of his command.

So, too, Marlow becomes for Lord Jim "an ally, a helper, an accomplice" (p. 93). The ache for human contact, for a sharing of solitudes, is the novel's obsession. "I don't know how old I appeared to him—and how much wise," Marlow observes with pain. "Not half as old as I felt just then; not half as uselessly wise as I knew myself to be." And adds that he is drawn to Jim by more than "the fellowship of the craft," by the strength of "the feeling that binds a man to a child" (pp. 128, 129). Though all his people are orphans, Conrad remains one of the great portrayers of the anguished impotence of fatherhood. One of his great subjects is the frustration of maturity's useless generosity toward the young.

But Jim does more than frustrate Marlow. He also threatens him. In the traditional adventure bildungsroman the older man sets a standard of competence and bravery which the neophyte hero must try to match and which may thus become a measure of the young man's inadequacy. This is the pattern of the *Tremolino* adventure. But in *Lord Jim,* because Conrad's sense of his characters refuses to rest in the expected or the easy, the pattern is radically contorted, and it is the older man who discovers in the younger one a fearful measure of himself.

Marlow admits that his obsession with Jim's story, his passion "to go grubbing into the deplorable details" of Jim's act of cowardice, might seem like "an unhealthy curiosity." But he comes to understand even as he talks that "perhaps, unconsciously, I hoped I would find . . . something, some profound and redeeming cause, some merciful explanation, some convincing shadow of an excuse" (p. 50). His desperate fascination with Jim's career, his repeated intercessions on Jim's behalf after the Inquiry, and his confessions of bafflement and failure at the task of understanding and, still more, of telling about Jim —all this, Marlow comes hesitantly to realize, is a consequence of much more than a compassionate elder's sympathy for the plight of a younger fellow sailor. In a moment of particular insight, Marlow asks the decisive question: "Was it for my own sake that I wished to find some shadow of an excuse for that young fellow whom I had never seen before?" (p. 51).

For his own sake, of course: the older man's struggle with the meaning of Jim's history is, in a sense, a struggle for moral survival. This is so for two reasons, both of which issue from the fact that Marlow is a clear if complex embodiment of the type of the sailor-teacher. First, because Jim is "one of us," his cowardice might have been Marlow's own. As Brierly's suicide shows, Jim threatens even the best of sailors because he represents, in Guerard's phrase, "an unsuspected potential self." [23] Later, as Guerard and others have observed, Jim himself will suffer from a similar crippling identification with Gentleman Brown:

> And there ran through the rough talk a vein of subtle reference to their common blood, an assumption of common experience; a sickening suggestion of common guilt, of secret knowledge that was like a bond of their minds and of their hearts. [p. 387]

But Marlow is more aware of a second reason for his anguished and intimate involvement with Jim, and the fact that this second motive is a conscious one does not render it any less compelling. For if Marlow can unearth no "merciful explanation," no "redeeming cause" for Jim's cowardice, he will be forced to admit that the commitments of his lifetime have been a mockery. "Haven't I," this sailor-teacher muses with a cloying heartiness he will largely abandon as his obsession with the act of telling Jim's story intensifies,

> Haven't I turned out youngsters enough in my time . . . The sea has been good to me, but when I remember all these boys that passed through my hands, some grown up now and some drowned by this time, but all good stuff for the sea, I don't think I have done badly by it either. Were I to go home tomorrow, I bet that before two days passed over my head some sunburnt young chief mate would overtake me at some dock gateway or other, and a fresh deep voice speaking above my hat would ask: "Don't you remember me, sir? Why! little So-and-so. Such and such a ship. It was my first voyage." [p. 44]

Marlow's sense of himself and his worth is intimately tied to his commitment to the job of initiating young men into the craft of the sea. He is a more serious and more responsible Dominic Cervoni, fully conscious of the crucially sustaining values embodied in the fellowship between master-sailor and apprentice:

> By-and-by, when [the young man] has learned all the little mysteries and the one great secret of the craft, he shall be fit to live or die as the sea may decree; and the man who had taken a hand in this fool game . . . will be pleased to have his back slapped by a heavy young hand, and to hear a cheery sea-puppy voice: "Do you remember me, sir? The little So-and-so."
>
> I tell you this is good; it tells you that once in your life

at least you had gone the right way to work. I have been thus slapped, and I have winced, for the slap was heavy, and I have glowed all day long and gone to bed feeling less lonely in the world by virtue of that hearty thump. [p. 45]

Marlow's forced gruffness in this passage poignantly signals his unease at the prospect of articulating the convictions that justify his career as a sailor and his life as a man. He feels "less lonely" having re-met his former apprentice, because in that meeting a continuity between generations is affirmed, and because, too, his past community with "little So-and-so" is briefly revived. In that former time the young man and Marlow his teacher had joined together in what Conrad elsewhere calls "the shared solitude of the sea" (*Tales of Unrest*, p. 26), and in this sharing had briefly overcome the intolerable isolation which presses like a plague upon Marlow, as upon so many Conrad characters.

Since Marlow believes that his life makes sense because, as a sailor and teacher of sailors, he has entered into and helped to preserve a community of men and of craft, Jim's desertion of the *Patna* profoundly threatens him. Jim might have been any one of the young so-and-so's whose training into seamanship and manhood has been the business of Marlow's life:

> He was the kind of fellow you would, on the strength of his looks, leave in charge of the deck—figuratively and professionally speaking. I say I would, and I ought to know. Haven't I turned out youngsters enough in my time . . . I tell you I ought to know the right kind of looks. I would have trusted . . . that youngster on the strength of a single glance, and gone to sleep with both eyes—and, by Jove! it wouldn't have been safe. There are depths of horror in that thought. [pp. 44, 45]

It is a small enough faith to hold to the notion that one's practiced eye can distinguish between reliable and unreliable men, but it is a faith necessary to such a man as Marlow. If he can be mistaken about Jim, then he could have been mistaken about every one of his other young men. This hard truth contains "depths of horror" not because it undermines Marlow's confidence in his ability to judge a man—that is a mere blow to one's self-esteem, and can be borne—but because there can be no partnership in hazard if your companion is not to be trusted. To lose one's partner is to confront what Decoud, bereft of *his* partner, confronts on the Golfo Placido: the dissolution of human community and (therefore) the dissolution of the self. Jim's desertion of an imperiled humanity, that is to say, exposes as fraudulent, as mere illusion, that sustaining partnership of "shared solitude" between sailors, that fellowship of trust and mutual effort whose existence is, for Marlow and also for Conrad, one of the "few simple notions you must cling to"—I am quoting Marlow—"if you want to live decently and would like to die easy" (*Lord Jim,* p. 43).

Once we have understood in all its fullness and pressing seriousness the nature of Marlow's involvement with Jim, the full import of the novel's digressive, apparently fragmented structure becomes clear. Guerard is surely correct when he observes that Marlow's "deceptive casualness of manner" minimizes the unfavorable evidence against Jim: "He is a considerably more lenient witness than his austere moralizing tone suggests. On various occasions he brings in the damaging evidence . . . very casually and digressively, as though inviting us to overlook it." [24] Jim's career inspires Marlow to several acts of insight and eloquence, but none, perhaps, so relevant as this famous sentence to the evasive, dodging form of the story Marlow himself has constructed: "It is my belief that no man ever understands quite his own artful dodges to escape from the grim shadow of self-knowledge" (p. 80). Marlow's dodges—like Conrad's in *A Personal Record*—are indeed artful, more artful than Jim's own and, I should say, more worthy; and surely it is clear that he is moved to such impressionist strategies in good part because he is himself mortally implicated in Jim's fate.

If Marlow is the wise elder in *Lord Jim,* he is the young hero in "Youth" and *Heart of Darkness.* In this role Marlow closely resembles Jim himself, the protagonists of "The Secret Sharer" and *The Shadow-Line,* and the biographical Conrad as he appears in a series of moving and subtle encounters with senior officers, maritime examiners, and older relatives and companions in both *The Mirror of the Sea* and *A Personal Record.* In all these works, and in others, too, Conrad studies his fundamental subject—the continuities and distances between youth and age, showing us wise elders, and some not so wise, attempting to pass on their knowledge (or sometimes their madness) to younger men, and showing us younger men as sometimes eager, sometimes hostile learners. In the best of these books Conrad projects a world very like Wordsworth's, in which we discover our saving connections with the human community almost by accident and in the least likely of men.

The central figures in these works share with Stevenson's protagonists and with John Kemp natures that are untested and eager for adventure, yet Conrad achieves freshness by emphasizing the enormous distance between the young man's visions of what his experience will be like and the sordid reality he actually encounters. Even in "Youth," where the interest, in some measure like that of the conventional adventure yarn, remains fixed on externals, Conrad pushes past the stereotype by stressing the idea that youth's self-involvement has in it an aspect of

near-cruelty, for the relatively easy comedy of the story is
deepened at those moments when young Marlow's obsession with his own adventure blinds him to the pathos of
old Captain Beard, struggling so futilely with an ill-favored first command that has come to him too late and
aboard an unsound vessel. In "Youth," too, it must be
said, the young hero is not so piously respected as his
counterpart in the conventional adventure voyage. As I
mentioned in an earlier chapter, Marlow's ironically nos-
talgic apostrophes to youth strike me as forced and sentimental, but he is more successful when he restrains his
impulse to generalize and just tells his story. When he
does this, the disparity between what his younger self
makes of his experiences and the reality old Marlow describes is genuinely comic and achieves the affectionate
deflation he wants but does not get in his more "philosophic" asides:

> We pumped watch and watch, for dear life; and it seemed
> to last for months, for years, for all eternity, as though we
> had been dead and gone to a hell for sailors. . . . The
> sails blew away, she lay broadside on under a weather-
> cloth, the ocean poured over her, and we did not care.
> We turned those handles, and had the eyes of idiots. As
> soon as we had crawled on deck I used to take a round
> turn with a rope about the men, the pumps, and the
> mainmast, and we turned, we turned incessantly, with the
> water to our waists, to our necks, over our heads. It was
> all one. We had forgotten how it felt to be dry.
>   And there was somewhere in me the thought: By Jove!
> this is the deuce of an adventure—something you read
> about. [pp. 11–12]

"Youth" remains, of course, a charming but uncompli-
cated story, and it may be that it lacks the resonant depths
of works like *Lord Jim, Heart of Darkness* and *The Shadow-Line* in part because Conrad's departures from the ad-

venture model in this early piece are fairly minimal. In "Youth," moreover, Conrad gives but scant attention to the adventure partnership, that drama of fraternity he most richly exploits elsewhere in his work. Mahon, young Marlow's fellow officer, shares jokes with his friend but neither threatens nor teaches him. And Captain Beard seems old and foolish and irrelevant to young Marlow, blinkered as he is by his romantic immaturity and incapable of understanding the older man's disquieting example. This theme itself is a particularly rich one for Conrad, and he examines it more directly in *The Shadow-Line*, perhaps his subtlest adventure story, where the young man's indifference to the figure of the experienced senior becomes in the opening scene with Captain Giles active resistance to the older man's efforts to help him.

Giles is a distant cousin to Dominic Cervoni, for both men are types of the wise elder whose task it is to help to initiate the young hero into the burdens and perils of responsible maturity. But in *The Shadow-Line* the exterior simplicities of the type have been wholly discarded. Giles is a garrulous, placid, and slightly pompous old captain "with a great shiny dome of a bald forehead and prominent brown eyes," who seems to the narrator "anything but a seaman" (p. 11). That his appearance contrasts so drastically with Dominic's vigorous and piratical demeanor, not to mention the tattooed glamor of the heroes in Conrad's late novels, simply indicates that Conrad is in control of the essentials of the convention, that he is using the convention and not being used by it. For Giles remains a man of great nautical experience, an "expert in . . . intricate navigation" who is reputed "to know more about remote and imperfectly charted parts of the Archipelago than any man living" (p. 12). In the *Tremolino* episode, the young hero's admiration for his experienced partner makes him a willing student, but in the subtler

Shadow-Line the narrator discovers the companions who will sustain and teach him only despite himself. Moreover, as Ian Watt has demonstrated in his fine essay on this story, the lessons the young hero finally learns, both from Giles and later from Ransome and the rest of his crew, are more complex than the relatively simple example of courage and skill which Dominic sets for the young Conrad. Finally, unlike the simple adventure story whose conclusion is always decisively clear, *The Shadow-Line,* as Watt reminds us, ends with "no heroic finality; and in the narrator's last interview with Giles we can find no warrant for believing that the shadow-line is crossed once and forever: we are never . . . in the clear; nor are the forces of inertia ever wholly vanquished." [25]

Yet such departures are fully resonant exactly because they are departures: the very subtlety of the story depends in good part upon Conrad's wrenching of the conventional stereotypes. For in the wry incisive comedy of the opening scene, the wise elder in effect forces his wisdom upon a bored and disrespectful junior, whose indifference nearly causes him to lose his first command. And later, as the neophyte captain parts from Giles to assume his command, that benevolent and "paternal" fellow seaman predicts the coming ordeal—"I expect you'll have your hands pretty full of tangled up business" (p. 43)—finally pressing upon the young captain the unwanted advice which will in the end be his salvation:

> "The Gulf . . . Ay! A funny piece of water—that," said Captain Giles. . . .
>
> I didn't inquire as to the nature of that funniness. . . . But at the very last he volunteered a warning.
>
> "Whatever you do keep to the east side of it. The west side is dangerous at this time of the year. Don't let anything tempt you over. You'll find nothing but trouble there." [pp. 44–45; first ellipsis Conrad's]

The narrator of *The Shadow-Line* has need of another partner once he has embarked on his voyage, and this partner, like Giles, is superficially unlike the traditional adventure retainer. No romantic outlaw with a maimed leg like Long John Silver or a cutlassed forearm like Thomas Castro, this figure's disablement is internal: he is Ransome, the ship's cook, and he has a bad heart. But in the great crisis aboard ship, with the entire crew struck down by fever, Ransome is a prodigy of energy and endurance; he becomes the embodiment of the indispensable man, "unfailing" (p. 105) and faithful, the "consummate seaman" (p. 126) who "noticed everything, attended to everything, shed comfort around him as he moved" (p. 121). And like the traditional loyal retainer, Ransome's sustaining presence rescues the hero himself. In his moment of greatest doubt—"I always suspected I might be no good"—the narrator discovers Ransome lingering in his cabin

> as if he had something to do there, but hesitated about doing it. I said suddenly:
> "You think I ought to be on deck?"
> He answered at once but without any particular emphasis or accent: "I do, sir."
> I got to my feet briskly, and he made way for me to go out. [pp. 107–08]

Like John Kemp, who comes to realize that without Castro he and Seraphina "should have died from exposure and exhaustion" (*Romance,* p. 363), the narrator of *The Shadow-Line* acknowledges his debt to Ransome: "I don't know what we should have done without [him]" (p. 122). "I, and the ship, and everyone on board of her, are very much indebted to you" (p. 123). But this debt, of course, is credible as Kemp's can never be, and it involves not only Ransome's consummate seamanship but also his other work as a moral savior.

In the ship's final desperate run into port only the captain and Ransome are able to sail the vessel, and in this vision of two men struggling together to survive calamity and further bound in a fraternity of weakness—Ransome's weak heart the physical emblem of his captain's moral incertitude—lies one of Conrad's recurring and deepest metaphors. In *The Shadow-Line* the rest of the crew lies helpless and semi-conscious on the decks as these partners in adventure work alone to save them. Earlier, the story has provided a comic prefiguring of this climactic moment when Giles, in the scene in the sailors' home, attempts to protect the narrator from the petty hostilities and machinations of the house steward. In *Typhoon* Jukes and his captain, contending with the fierce hostility of the storm, are thrown together in a literal embrace which symbolizes this same vision of human partnership besieged and in danger but finally surviving. And in a similar way, Dominic and the young Conrad aboard the *Tremolino,* in flight from enemies and betrayed by one of their fellows, must confer in secret about their betrayal and remain silent lest their unwilling crew mutiny rather than risk the perils of escape. In all these moments, and consummately in *Heart of Darkness,* Conrad wrests from the conventional adventure partnership an enduring image of human community collapsed to its very limits and threatened, though not always undone, by annihilation.

Both Captain Beard and Giles, like Jim's Marlow, are benign figures, the one at worst unaware of his younger officer's need for instruction, the other actively seeking to help him. In *Heart of Darkness* and in "The Secret Sharer" this kindly fellow is radically transformed and, though inescapably the hero's accomplice and partner, becomes also his enemy. Our communion extends, Words-

worth tells us in poems like "Michael," or "The Old
Cumberland Beggar" or "The Idiot Boy," to the very
edges of the human, to old men walking who seem
scarcely alive, to leech-gatherers who are allied more
closely to inanimate nature than to our human quickness.
Just so, says Conrad in *Heart of Darkness* and "The Secret
Sharer," our communion extends, whether we like it or
not, even to murderers.

In both stories Conrad—like Stevenson before him in
such works as *The Master of Ballantrae* (1889), *The Ebb-
Tide* (1894), and his unfinished masterpiece *Weir of Her-
miston* (posthumously published in 1896)—manipulates
to brilliant advantage one of the easy, central common-
places of the adventure tradition: the wearying insistence
on the retainer figure's lawless demeanor and past. Conrad's own treatment of such characters as Peyrol and Lingard produces the type with sorry precision, and his handling of Castro and especially Dominic Cervoni shows
how he is able to use the convention effectively in its traditional outlines.

All these characters share with Kurtz and with Leggatt
the condition of an outlaw, and it is by virtue of that condition that they fascinate and appeal to the young men
who look upon them. If the wise, kindly elder—the Marlow of *Lord Jim,* Giles, the young Conrad's several captains in *The Mirror of the Sea*—is one version of the adventure retainer, a second version is what Leslie Fiedler
in a suggestive essay on Stevenson alternately calls "the
Beloved Scoundrel" and the "appealing rogue." That neither rogue nor scoundrel is a term adequate to Leggatt or
to Kurtz measures the full extent of Conrad's reshaping of
the Stevensonian stereotype. But Kurtz and Long John
Silver have common origins that bear fundamentally upon
Conrad's characteristic way of finding true fictions in the
worn materials of a popular genre. In a passage describing

Long John Silver's fascination, Fiedler might as easily be defining the relationship between the young Conrad and Dominic Cervoni, or between John Kemp and Thomas Castro:

> Long John Silver is described through a boy's eye, the first of those fictional first-person singulars who are a detached aspect of the author. It is Jim Hawkins who is the chief narrator of the tale, as it is Jim who saves the Sea-Cook from the gallows. For the boy, the scoundrel par excellence is the Pirate: an elemental ferocity belonging to the unfamiliar sea and uncharted islands hiding blood-stained gold. Vain, cruel, but astonishingly courageous and without self-doubt, able to compel respect, obedience, and even love—that is John Silver.[26]

Allowing for all differences in scale and intensity, we might also legitimately alter the final phrase to read, *that is Marlow's Kurtz.* Conrad's letter to Blackwood in defense and vindication of his art seems especially apt here, and his remarks about "Youth"—I quoted them earlier and must repeat them now—apply in some measure to *Heart of Darkness:*

> The favourable critics . . . remarked with a sort of surprise "This after all is a story for boys yet—"
> Exactly. Out of the material of a boys' story I've made *Youth* by the force of the idea expressed in accordance with a strict conception of my method.[27]

Kurtz is the bogey-man of the child's dream, at once repellent and attractive, transformed into the primitive near-demon of true nightmare. The nightmare is arresting and true because it takes place in a landscape whose weird concreteness is unforgettably vivid and because the demon has credible embodiments in the irrational turbulence of the interior life—"It is his extremity that I seem to have lived through" (p. 151)—and also in the external realities of the imperialist adventure—"All Europe contributed to the making of Kurtz" (p. 117). As the boy responds with a mingling of fear and admiration to the example of the powerful outlaw, so Kurtz's followers are inspired to respect, obedience, and grim ecstasies of devotion. Marlow is but one of these followers. There are, also, the worshiping natives to whom Kurtz has become one of the gods of the land. And there is the harlequin disciple who has nursed Kurtz through two illnesses and whose "devotion" to his master is clearly the "most dangerous" and least rational of all the hazardous commitments of his life. Like the relationship between the boy and his pirate-accomplice in the conventional Stevensonian pattern, the partnership between Kurtz and his disciple is an unequal one: "It was curious to see his mingled eagerness and reluctance to speak of Kurtz. The man filled his life, occupied his thoughts, swayed his emotions" (p. 128).

Not the least of the ironies in *Heart of Darkness* is Marlow's blindness to the fact that his comments about Kurtz's harlequin exactly describe his own response to Kurtz and to the task of telling about him. His evasive narrative, as Guerard has shown,[28] approaches Kurtz only reluctantly, postponing the climactic encounter with obsessive ingenuity. Like the harlequin, Marlow, his life filled with Kurtz, is yet "jealous of sharing with any one the peculiar blackness of that experience" (p. 142). And his partnership with the demon is a real one—as he explicitly acknowledges many times in his telling—demanding a loyalty far more perilous than that between partners in conventional adventure. "I accepted this unforeseen partnership," Marlow says, "this choice of nightmares," and moments later admits that "I have remained loyal to Kurtz to the last" (pp. 147, 151).

For part of the journey, on the trip back up river on his ancient steamer, Marlow is bound to the dying Kurtz in a

kinship ignored and distrusted by the other "pilgrims,"
who look upon Marlow now with "disfavour." "I was,
so to speak, numbered with the dead." During this
time Marlow holds in his hands "all that had been Kurtz's
. . . : his soul, his body, . . . his plans, his ivory, his car-
reer" (pp. 147, 155). And in these days of isolated communion Marlow and Kurtz enact together a terrible drama of
human fellowship. It is a fragile and imperiled fellowship,
threatened by the hostile pilgrims and by the warlike natives dancing along the shore; and undermined still more
by Kurtz's depraved hallucinations of power and grandeur
and by Marlow's fear and contempt for this "hollow
sham." But its intensely fragile, precarious nature also signals the desperate vigor of those human needs which call
such fraternity into life:

> I looked ahead—piloting. "Close the shutter," said Kurtz
> suddenly one day; "I can't bear to look at this." I did
> so. . . .
>
> One morning he gave me a packet of papers and a
> photograph—the lot tied together with a shoe-string.
> "Keep this for me," he said. . . .
>
> One evening coming in with a candle I was startled to
> hear him say a little tremulously, "I am lying here in the
> dark waiting for death." The light was within a foot of
> his eyes. I forced myself to murmur, "Oh, nonsense!" and
> stood over him as if transfixed. [pp. 148–49]

It is a radical and profound vision of community, reduced
as so often in Conrad to the smallest possible unit and imperiled, as I have said, by many things. But still it survives. Marlow is moved, partly by inner necessity, to com-
passion and even devotion, and Kurtz to asking
tremulously for them. Like Leggatt and the young captain
of "The Secret Sharer," but with even greater difficulty,
Kurtz and Marlow are partners in a great adventure

which measures the hero against an outlaw-accomplice, a companion in hazard of whom the hero must finally say, with Kurtz's harlequin, "Oh, he enlarged my mind!" (p. 140).

Conrad's unending interest in this drama of unexpected fraternity, in these rituals of sharing and continuity that are sometimes chosen, more often forced upon us, exposes the stoic, earthbound side of his art, a side of his work more important and central than the anarchic, exotic elements to be found in the Russian maelstrom of *Under Western Eyes* or in the ambiguous, savage, but also hollow transcendence achieved by Kurtz in *Heart of Darkness*. This pragmatic, profoundly Wordsworthian side of Conrad is perhaps distilled for us in the remark recorded by Edward Garnett which I quoted early in these pages: "Yes, dear Edward. But have you ever had to keep an enraged negro armed with a razor from coming aboard, along a ten-inch plank, and drive him back to the wharf with only a short stick in your hands?"[29]

Subjecting the exotic (and innocent) imagination to the test of real experience, this remark illuminates Conrad's characteristic revision of the typical adventure plot. The hero in conventional adventure, escaping the confines of the ordinary world, escapes also from his human limitations. In Conradian adventure, of course, the hero, "housed in a dream at distance from the Kind" like the younger self Wordsworth describes in *Peele Castle*, escapes into an unfamiliar universe only to be confronted with the fact of his error and weakness, with the sure and terrible limitations of his humanity, and with his need for other men.

Jim dreams of a "stirring life in a world of adventure" but learns in his leap from the *Patna* something, though not enough, of his true nature. The Marlow who tracks Kurtz into the wilderness sets out on his journey as if fulfilling a childhood dream of adventure—"I would put my finger on [the map's uncharted spaces] . . . and say, When I grow up I will go there" (*Heart of Darkness,* p. 52)—but the trip becomes a most private and "weary pilgrimage amongst hints for nightmares" (p. 62). Kurtz himself goes into the heart of darkness armed with moral ideas, only to discover in himself primitive longings and the final horror. The untried captain in "The Secret Sharer" takes his command "rejoic[ing] in the great security of the sea" which presents (he believes) "no disquieting problems" (*'Twixt Land and Sea,* p. 96), but comes to learn in his communion with a murderer-self that the sea's security is an illusion and that he is "not living in a boy's adventure tale" (p. 131). And finally, in *The Shadow-Line,* another young captain similarly longs for "the freedom of the great waters" in the full confidence of his sailor's knowledge—"One is a seaman or one is not. And I had no doubt of being one" (p. 44)—believing naively that those wide waters are "the only remedy for all my troubles" (p. 71), but comes to imagine that he has been "decoyed into this awful, this death-haunted command" (p. 98) and to "understand that strange sense of insecurity in my past. I always suspected that I might be no good. And here is positive proof, I am shirking it, I am no good" (p. 107).

From these inevitable disillusionments Conrad turns, as Wordsworth does, to such consolation as there is in what the Russian zealots of *Under Western Eyes* are said to scorn: "the irremediable life of the earth as it is"—and to what Dennis Donoghue has called "the ordinary universe." [30] This is a place in which elemental necessities join men to one another, a place in which men are not entirely cut off from their kind, because they share similar feelings, fear death and want to keep living, ally themselves together when they must, and carry on long conti-

nuities of labor and struggle. In such an earthbound
world, the poet or novelist discovers that one of his central
tasks is to preserve in the memory of other men what he
and those he has known have felt and have done. Conrad praises Frederick Marryat on these grounds, the loss
of whose books

> would be irreparable, like . . . the loss of a historical doc-
> ument. . . . History preserves the skeleton of facts and,
> here and there, a figure or a name; but it is in Marryat's
> novels that we find the mass of the nameless, that we see
> them in the flesh, that we obtain a glimpse of the every-
> day life and an insight into the spirit animating the
> crowd of obscure men who knew how to build for their
> country such a shining monument of memories. ["Tales
> of the Sea," *Notes on Life and Letters,* pp. 53–54]

And Conrad sees his own writing in terms of this documentary and commemorative mission. "What is a novel,"
he writes in *A Personal Record,* "if not a conviction of
our fellow-men's existence strong enough to take upon itself a form of imagined life clearer than reality and whose
accumulated verisimilitude of selected episodes puts to
shame the pride of documentary history" (p. 15). And,
again, in a more directly confessional and also more memorable passage from the same book:

> After all these years, each leaving its evidence of slowly
> blackened pages, I can honestly say that it is a sentiment
> akin to piety which prompted me to render in words as-
> sembled with conscientious care the memory of things far
> distant and of men who had lived. [p. 10]

A similar piety lies behind Wordsworth's special interest in beggars and wanderers, in leech-gatherers and solitary reapers. The reaping girl is a symbol, enigmatic and
rich, of elemental human continuities. Geoffrey Hartman
has written of this commemorative aspect of Wordsworth's

verse, linking his characteristic poems with a form of writing called the nature-inscription, in which natural objects and man-made ones like tombs or statues are inscribed with verses intended to memorialize some human or natural event.[31] Many of Wordsworth's lengthy titles suggest a similar specifying or commemorating impulse. "Lines left upon a Seat in a Yew-Tree, which stands near the Lake of Esthwaite, on a desolate part of the shore, yet commanding a beautiful prospect." "Elegiac Stanzas, suggested by a picture of Peele Castle, in a storm, painted by Sir George Beaumont." "Lines Composed a Few Miles above Tintern Abbey, on revisiting the banks of the Wye during a tour, July 13, 1789." The charming, extravagant particularity of such titles answers in part Wordsworth's deep need to mark, to preserve, the experiences he describes. The emotional states evoked in the poems draw sustaining weight and credibility from the earthbound precision of these titles. I felt this, Wordsworth says, at this particular place, two miles from that place, on this particular day in this particular year.

Conrad's extended effort "to make us see," to give us characters who (as he said in the splendid letter I quoted earlier) "will bleed to a prick, and are moving in a visible world" [32] parallels this Wordsworthian precision. And so does his compulsive need, in the prefaces to his novels, to insist on the real, autobiographical or historical origins of his stories and his characters. Don't disbelieve these characters, Conrad almost pleads with us in these author's notes. They really existed, I knew them, or read about them; or—sometimes—I *am* these characters. For Conrad the Wordsworthian attempt "to make unfamiliar things credible," to write with a clarity and a concreteness that would "envelop" his people and his settings "in their proper atmosphere of actuality" was "the hardest task of all and the most important" (Author's Note, *Within the*

Tides, p. vi). The powerful, recurring note of elegy in both Conrad and Wordsworth is part of this impulse to set down, to preserve, experiences or insights or stories that would otherwise be lost.

This impulse to memorialize and to connect things far distant and men who have lived is explicitly acknowledged in the preface to the *Lyrical Ballads* and in many places in Conrad's nonfiction, most notably in his preface to *The Nigger of the "Narcissus."* Near the conclusion of that famous but carelessly read essay, Conrad elaborates a surprising definition of the artist. In an extended analogy, he compares the writer to "a labourer in a distant field" whose exertions are at once ordinary and vaguely mysterious. We who observe this laborer, Conrad says, are not desperate to understand him; our attention to his work is accidental, a leisurely interval as we lie "stretched at ease in the shade of a roadside tree." But "after a time," Conrad continues, we may

> begin to wonder languidly as to what the fellow may be at. We watch the movements of his body, the waving of his arms, we see him bend down, stand up, hesitate, begin again. . . . If we know he is trying to lift a stone, to dig a ditch, to uproot a stump, we look with a more real interest at his efforts; we are disposed to condone the jar of his agitation upon the restfulness of the landscape; and even, if in a brotherly frame of mind, we may bring ourselves to forgive his failure. We understood his object, and, after all, the fellow has tried, and perhaps he had not the strength—and perhaps he had not the knowledge. We forgive, go on our way—and forget.
>
> And so it is with the workman of art. [p. xi]

This passage deserves more attention than it seems to have received from Conrad's readers and critics; and our failure to take account of its implications seems the more remarkable since the preface to *The Nigger of the "Narcissus"* has been so often quoted and reprinted. Although the preface as a whole is usually understood as a manifesto of modernism, the passage I have quoted seems scarcely to fit our expectations for a modern theory of fiction.

The odd mingling of pessimism and charity that marks the passage is clearly more purely Conradian than modern. So too is the disquieting modesty—it is perhaps just honest realism—implicit in the assumption that literature is an activity that engages most men only in their leisure moments. More centrally, the very terms of Conrad's analogy have an old-fashioned, distinctly "unmodern" character. For Conrad's comparison of the writer to a worker in a field, his identification of ordinary human work with the enterprise of art, runs counter to symbolist and postsymbolist notions of the artist as a man isolated from his fellow men, relying (like Joyce's artist-hero) on silence, exile, and cunning to get his work done. Resisting the idea of the artist's alienation, grounding itself instead in an unstrident sense that we all belong to a fraternity of failure, the Conrad passage is not easily compatible with such (by now) standard versions of the role of art and the artist as these, which I take from the table of contents of Ellmann and Feidelson's *The Modern Tradition:* "Art as Ascetic Religion" (Flaubert), "The Poet as Revolutionary Seer" (Rimbaud), "Art as Aristocratic Mystery" (Mallarmé), "Poetry as a Game of Knowledge" (Auden).

If we look to place Conrad's laborer in more congenial company, we must go back to the Romantics and particularly, of course, to Wordsworth. The passage I have quoted, in fact, is something near to a prose paraphrase of that recurring Wordsworth lyric in which a halted traveler looks across a rural distance at another human figure who is bent to the landscape, doing the work of survival.

Acknowledging the physical and other distances that separate him from the figure he is observing, the watcher's meditation (like Conrad's paragraph) is at the same time an assertion of the bonds between them; and however weighted with a sense of loss or partialness, it is an act of community.

These parallels are scarcely fortuitous, for there is a definitive kinship between the whole of Conrad's preface and Wordsworth's earlier, more systematic one. Both distinguish art from science, both speak of the need to revitalize a language that has (in Conrad's words) been "defaced by ages of careless usage." Both affirm art as a bringer of truth. But their most important agreement is their joint definition of the artist's mission.

The poet, says Wordsworth, is one "who binds together by passion and knowledge the vast empire of human society, as it is spread over the whole earth, and over all time." Conrad's version of this troubles the modern ear, and emphasizes the specially Romantic virtue of sincerity:

> To snatch in a moment of courage, from the remorseless rush of time, a passing phase of life, is only the beginning of the task. The task approached in tenderness and faith is to hold up unquestioningly, without choice and without fear, the rescued fragment before all eyes in the light of a sincere mood. It is to show its vibration, its colour, its form; and through its movement, its form, and its colour, reveal the substance of its truth—disclose its inspiring secret: the stress and passion within the core of each convincing moment. In a single-minded attempt of that kind, if one be deserving and fortunate, one may perchance attain to such clearness of sincerity that at last the presented vision of regret or pity, of terror or mirth, shall awaken in the hearts of the beholders that feeling of unavoidable solidarity; of the solidarity in mysterious origin, in toil, in joy, in hope, in uncertain fate, which

binds men to each other and all mankind to the visible world. [p. x]

I find even the ornateness of that statement moving, and yet another measure of Conrad's decisive allegiances with the century of Wordsworth.

Epilogue

Conrad and Modern English Fiction

T. S. Eliot borrowed famously from *Heart of Darkness* in his epigraph to "The Hollow Men": *Mistah Kurtz—he dead*. And however serviceable this borrowing may have been, it can also be said to crystallize the partial and limiting view of Conrad's work that this book has wished to qualify. To insist, as I have tried to do, on the way in which Conrad's major fiction describes and deeply values our fragile but genuine human connections is not to deny Conrad his melancholy. But it is to imply that the largely unqualified despair in Eliot's early poetry constitutes a special rather than a representative instance of the modernist imagination. Indeed, as I read and reread Conrad, fortifying my sense of his deep sympathies with that anti-apocalyptic strain in Romanticism that Lionel Trilling describes in "Wordsworth and the Rabbis"[1] and that is dramatized so powerfully in poems like Wordsworth's "Tintern Abbey" and Keats's "To Autumn," I came increasingly to see that my notions about Conrad could be applied in some degree to James and to the major English novelists who immediately follow them.

There is a large irony in the fact that our revised understanding of the intimate links between the Romantics and the early modern poets has not been extended to the novelists of the same period. We have come to see that despite their aggressive insistence on their own distance from the nineteenth century, the modern poets were the heirs and continuers of the very tradition they claimed to subvert. But the related notion that the central figures in the great modern novels may not be counterparts of J. Alfred Prufrock has yet to be widely acknowledged.

Though other influences are also involved, it is a remarkable tribute to Eliot's immense authority that the prevailing understanding of modern fiction should continue to center on the themes of barrenness and despair. In the famous review of *Ulysses*—paradoxically, an effort to defend Joyce's book from Richard Aldington's attack on its alleged perversity and formlessness—Eliot praises what he calls Joyce's "mythical method": a method, he says, that gives shape and significance "to the immense panorama of futility and anarchy that is contemporary history." [2] This is not, of course, a neutral critical description but a signal instance of a writer-critic reading his own practices and perceptions into the work of another. Embedded in Eliot's sentence, as in the essay as a whole, is the assumption that Joyce shared his sense of the world's "futility" and that Joyce's technical innovations embody just such a hopeless and crisis-ridden view. This association of technical innovativeness with a vision of despair dominated the Joyce scholarship until fairly recently, and continues, I think, to be largely characteristic of the general attitude toward writers like Conrad, Woolf, and Ford Madox Ford.

Gloom and apocalypse are, in any case, recurring themes for some of the most important critics of modern fiction. Erich Auerbach, for example, at the conclusion of what remains perhaps the single most impressive analysis of the essential techniques of modern fiction, speaks of the "air of vague and hopeless sadness" in Virginia Woolf's novels, of Joyce's "blatant and painful cynicism," of a "certain atmosphere of universal doom" and "hopelessness" that pervades modernist fiction generally.[3] And Irving Howe, a consistent and important champion of modernism, has repeatedly stressed its extremist and nihilistic impulses. "The 'modern,' " Howe summarizes in a recent book, "as it refers to both history and literature, signifies extreme situations and radical solutions. It summons images of war and revolution, experiment and disaster, apocalypse and skepticism; images of rebellion, disenchantment and nothingness." [4] Although this fearful catalogue may correspond in some degree to the work of Continental modernists, it seems to me to apply in the English tradition only to certain extremist and unrepresentative figures like the early Eliot.

Though I have no wish to deny modern fiction's recurring insistence on the radically problematic and even estranging aspects of experience, I cannot feel that Howe's, or Auerbach's, emphasis takes account of the powerfully antiapocalyptic temper of the great modern English novels, their shared respect for what Conrad calls "the irremediable life of the earth as it is." Ellmann's sense of this quality in Joyce has a brilliant conciseness: "Joyce's discovery, so humanistic that he would have been embarrassed to disclose it out of context, was that the ordinary is the extraordinary." [5] This Joycean impulse to recover and to celebrate the ordinary has roots deep in Romanticism, of course, and is widely shared not only by Conrad but by other modern English writers as well. It is central, for instance, in Ford, whose great and still undervalued tetralogy is in part a meditation on the antiapocalyptic character of our individual lives. Against a backdrop of the most decisive public and political events, *Parade's End* shows us characters whose natures change only minimally; and whose desire to alter or to transform themselves is satisfied only ambiguously and incompletely. (This is why Tietjens himself is largely absent from the pages of the concluding volume of the tetralogy, having been drawn away from his simple country retreat and his new life as an antique dealer back to Groby, the ancestral home from which he had imagined himself to be finally free.) Ford's largest theme, in fact, might be said to be the disjunction between the enormous political eruptions that the society he describes is experiencing and the far more minimal and ordinary alterations that occur in the lives of his characters. This theme is elaborated most fully in the career of his protagonist, who in the course of his education—*Parade's End,* like many of the great English novels of the period, is a *bildungsroman* but about an adult—must come to terms with the simplest and most elemental facts about himself, must acknowledge that he is unhappy, that being a Tietjens of Groby does not exempt him from pain or simple human need or even—during the war—ambition for advancement. This small and basic insight Ford sees as a remarkable act of will and moral heroism. Just so, I think, in Joyce, Bloom's increasing capacity simply to confront directly the fact of Molly's infidelity and his own partial responsibility for it is a crucial drama of the book. Bloom changes little in *Ulysses,* advances only to a rich equanimity concerning the partialness of life, and the novel insists in every possible way on the ordinariness and simplicity of his consolations.

This emphasis on the ordinary, the simple human thing, is crucial, too, in Virginia Woolf, who finds in the most elementary human gatherings and undertakings—parties, dinners, moments of intimacy in conversation, public pageants that draw people briefly out of their separateness—a fragile but real counterforce to the fact that time passes and nothing endures but the neutral indifferent sea.

Even Lawrence, who loves apocalypse, has a way of acknowledging, if only in his best books, the world's resistance to the imagination of crisis and transformation. Lawrence, it would seem to me, is in fact at his most Romantic in those books—*Women in Love* far above all—in which the spirit's yearning for transcendence is mocked and frustrated, so that Lawrence is then able, like the Romantic poets of the century before him, to tell the truth not only about the yearning but also about what really happens to it in the world. Birkin weeping before Gerald's corpse—he had earlier said one oughtn't to waste tears on the dead—and Birkin in the last pages of the novel, returned to the England, to the very roof, he had thought to put behind him in his journey into fullness—this Birkin lives in a partial, indecisive world of simple human intimacies that is not entirely at odds with the world of Joyce or Woolf or Ford Madox Ford.

One way of clarifying these matters is to suggest that J. Alfred Prufrock, or Gregor Samsa, is a far less characteristic modernist figure than James's Strether, who disembarks in Europe to find himself in a new world of overwhelming complexity and nuance. If traditional moral assumptions and old stabilities are called into question for Strether, and if he feels the loss of such assurances acutely, he is conscious at the same time of the challenge and the variousness of the world he has entered. His position is endangered and precarious, but he has much to see and little inclination to despair. Strether can serve, I think, as an emblem not only for many of the protagonists of modern English fiction but also for the makers of it: for their shared sense of the difficulties, even the terrors, but also the excitements of the world they wished to render in art.

The formulations about the nature of modern fiction offered us by Virginia Woolf and Ford Madox Ford seem to me far more accurate and helpful than Eliot's review of Joyce. In Woolf's two major essays on modern fiction and in the extended reflections on fictional technique scattered through Ford's memoirs and other books, there is a remarkable accord. Both writers suggest that life as they see and understand it had not been adequately rendered in earlier novels, largely because older fictional methods are called into question by the modern awareness of the complexities of the inner life and by a recognition of the ways in which one's subjective vision selects and colors experience. Both, in their own ways, and Conrad, James, Lawrence, and Joyce in theirs, tried to devise techniques that would do justice to the new complexity they saw before them. They are all, except for Lawrence, suspicious of apocalypse. "Let us not take it for granted," Woolf writes, echoing many passages in Ford, "that life exists more fully in what is commonly thought big than in what is commonly thought small." And they reject conventional versions of plot and of literary structure. Here is Woolf speaking, then Ford:

> Examine for a moment an ordinary mind on an ordinary day. The mind receives a myriad impressions—trivial, fantastic, evanescent, or engraved with the sharpness of steel. From all sides they come, an incessant shower of innumerable atoms; and as they fall, . . . the accent falls differently from of old; the moment of importance came not here but there; so that if a writer were a free man and not a slave, if he could write what he chose, . . . there would be no plot, no comedy, no tragedy, no love interest or catastrophe in the accepted style. . . . Life is not a series of gig lamps symmetrically arranged; but a luminous halo, a semi-transparent envelope surrounding us from the beginning of consciousness to the end. Is it not the task of the novelist to convey this varying, this unknown and uncircumscribed spirit, whatever aberration or complexity it may display, with as little mixture of the alien and external as possible? [6]

We agreed that the general effect of a novel must be the general effect that life makes on mankind. A novel must therefore not be a narration, a report. Life does not say to you: In 1914 my next door neighbour, Mr. Slack, erected a greenhouse and painted it with Cox's green aluminium paint. . . . If you think about the matter you will remember, in various unordered pictures, how one day Mr. Slack appeared in his garden and contemplated the wall of his house. You will then try to remember the year of that occurrence and you will fix it as August 1914 because having had the foresight to bear the municipal stock of the city of Liège you were able to afford a first-class season ticket for the first time in your life. You will remember Mr. Slack ... again [in] ... his garden, this time with a pale, weaselly-faced fellow, who touched his cap from time to time. Mr. Slack will point to his house-wall several times at different points, the weaselly fellow touching his cap at each pointing. Some days after, coming back from business you will have observed against Mr. Slack's wall. . . . At this point you will remember that you were then the manager of the fresh-fish branch of Messrs. Catlin and Clovis in Fenchurch Street. . . . What a change since then! Millicent had not yet put her hair up. . . . You will remember how Millicent's hair looked, rather pale and burnished in plaits. You will remember how it now looks, henna'd ... You remember some of the things said by means of which Millicent has made you cringe—and her expression! . . . Cox's Aluminium Paint! . . . You remember the half empty tin that Mr. Slack showed you ...

And, if that is how the building of your neighbour's greenhouse comes back to you, just imagine how it will be with your love-affairs that are so much more complicated. . . .[7]

Both passages seem to me remarkably clear explanations for the unconventional methods of modern fiction. Both adhere firmly to a mimetic conception of literature, appealing directly to the real world, to the way things are or seem to us to be. And in neither passage is there the suggestion that the complexity of this reality is a cue for

despair. The modern novelists realize, of course, that nihilism may be a logical consequence of the perception
that the world's significance is subjective and private, and
they give us characters—like Decoud, or Mr. Ramsay, or
Stephen Dedalus—who are tortured and sometimes destroyed by this recognition. But being novelists and not
metaphysicians they live with muddle and inconsistency
more readily than some of their characters, and their
"working assumptions," as Ian Watt has written of Conrad, "echo the greatest of English empiricists, who in
Twelfth Night gave Sir Andrew Aguecheek the immortal
words: 'I have no exquisite reason for 't, but I have reason
good enough.' " [8]

The harshness but also the beauty of modern fiction, its
tough honesty but also its odd exuberance, have an illuminating parallel in the writings of Freud. The Freud I
have in mind is the stoic humanist who emerges from
some of Lionel Trilling's essays and, most impressively,
from Philip Rieff's great book.[9] Like the modern novelists
who were, roughly, his contemporaries, this Freud is
aware of the definitive inwardness of men, of their
estrangement from themselves and from their fellows, of
the tyranny of the trivial and the quotidian. But, again
like the novelists, Freud's sense of our grave human
limits leads not to despair but to a recognition of man's
resilience and his capacity for that tough-minded candor
which can lead to a minimal self-mastery and even, sometimes, to a kind of secular reverence for things as they are:

> How [did Bloom enter the bed]?
> With circumspection, as invariably when entering an
> abode (his own or not his own): with solicitude, the snake-
> spiral springs of the mattress being old, the brass quoits
> and pendent viper radii loose and tremulous under stress
> and strain: prudently, as entering a lair or ambush of lust
> or adder: lightly, the less to disturb: reverently, the bed of

conception and of birth, of consummation of marriage
and of breach of marriage, of sleep and of death.

Both Freud and these writers speak in their different
ways especially of the essential human labor of perception,
of seeing the world and the self clearly. They are antago-
nistic to lies and deception. Warily, mainly by implication
and sometimes with terrible obliqueness the writers affirm
the tough-minded clarity of Mrs. Ramsay:

> It will end, it will end, she said. It will come, it will
> come, when suddenly she added, We are in the hands of
> the Lord.
> But instantly she was annoyed with herself for saying
> that. Who had said it? Not she; she had been trapped
> into saying something she did not mean. She looked up
> over her knitting . . . purifying out of existence that lie,
> any lie.

Freud's book about this particular lie, *The Future of an
Illusion* (1927), focuses, like the novelists, on the theme of
seeing and growing:

> True, man will then [having renounced religion] find
> himself in a difficult situation. He will have to confess his
> utter helplessness and his insignificant part in the work-
> ing of the universe; he will have to confess that he is no
> longer the centre of creation, no longer the object of the
> tender care of a benevolent providence. He will be in the
> same position as the child who has left the home where
> he was so warm and comfortable. But, after all, is it not
> the destiny of childishness to be overcome? Man cannot
> remain a child for ever; he must venture at last into the
> hostile world.[10]

That these generalizations are fitted to Conrad I think
is beyond question. Yet I would not insist on them too ex-
clusively. For there is something quaint, old-fashioned
about him, and one feels toward his work in some degree

as his friends seem to have felt about his person: that he
was uneasy not only in that place of exile whose language
he appropriated and greatly honored, but also in the time
in which he lived. There is a rich, simple nostalgia in
him, and a decorousness and reticence not at all modern.
He is different from Joyce and Woolf and his friend Ford,
even less at home with them, finally, than the older James.
The Singleton of modern literature, he stands nearer to
Wordsworth than to Joyce.

Something of his special quality may be suggested by
Walter Allen's distinction between two classes of novelists,
the sophisticated and the naive:

> The sophisticated novelist is one who is aware, in the fore-
> ground of his consciousness, of his special relation as
> novelist to his subject-matter or to his readers, often, in-
> deed, to both. The naive novelist, on the other hand, is
> much more plainly the lineal descendant of the primitive
> story-teller. He takes his audience's interest for granted; he
> knows they want to hear a story. "Take my word for it,
> this is the way it happened," is his attitude.[11]

What is striking about Conrad, of course, is the extent to
which he fits both of Allen's groupings. (So, too, he would
seem to unite both the "drama" and the "romance" of Stevenson's famous definition: "Drama is the poetry of conduct, romance the poetry of circumstance.") [12] It is
scarcely possible to imagine a more self-conscious writer
than Conrad, to imagine anyone more aware of his special
relation to his material and to his audience. Yet he is, like
any writer of adventure fiction, clearly descended from the
"primitive story-teller." Indeed, in *Lord Jim* and elsewhere both Conrad and Marlow presume upon and subtly
exploit their audience's patience: "In regard to the listeners' endurance," Conrad writes in an author's note, "the

postulate must be accepted that the story *was* interesting. It is the necessary preliminary assumption" (*Lord Jim*, p. vii).

Ford Madox Ford understood the mixed character of Conrad's fiction, and focused on it in a comparison between his collaborator and two of his famous contemporaries, James and Stephen Crane. James's people, Ford tells us, attend tea parties that are "debating circles of a splendid aloofness, of an immense human sympathy," while Crane is interested in

> physical life, in wars, in slums, in Western saloons, in a world where the "gun" was the final argument. The life that Conrad gives you is somewhere halfway between the two; it is dominated—but less dominated—by the revolver than that of Stephen Crane, and dominated, but less dominated, by the moral scruple than that of James.[13]

This judgment—like most of Ford's literary opinions—is particularly acute, for it is clear that in novel after novel Conrad tries to mingle the sophisticated and the primitive, tries to tell great old-fashioned stories complexly and fully. His subject matter is consistently that of the popular adventure story, his plots are nearly always potentially melodramatic, his rhetoric is always listing toward ornateness and excess. Yet his important work, far from succumbing to the simplification and banality inherent in these things, retrieves from them a rare and austere seriousness. And Conrad accomplishes this work of discovery and rescue, I hope the foregoing has shown, not by denying extravagance but by using it. Although, as I have argued, a principal concern of Conrad's narrative strategies is to deflect our attention away from such extravagance, his successful work never finally denies—is never finally afraid to make use of—the acts and gestures and circumstances that are characteristic of Stevenson and Kipling and Rider Haggard.

"I remember," writes Lionel Trilling, "with what a smile of saying something daring and inacceptable John Erskine told an undergraduate class that some day we would understand that plot and melodrama were good things for a novel to have and that *Bleak House* was a very good novel indeed." [14] One wants, I think, to say something of the same for Conrad, but with the emphasis upon his bloody combats and natural disasters, his pirate battles (as in the conclusion of *Lord Jim*) and his threatening seas (as in *Typhoon* and *The Shadow-Line*).

To say this is to reinforce Ford's estimate of Conrad, an estimate that implicitly clarifies Conrad's complex, mediating role in the development of modern fiction. Ford recalls that James described *Romance* as "an immense English Plum Cake which he kept at his bedside for a fortnight and of which he ate nightly a slice." [15] If James did not say that, he ought to have, for the remark's typically Jamesian mixture of courtesy and condescension suggests exactly how alien and "unserious" such a book must have appeared to the writer Conrad addressed in his letters as "très cher maître." [16]

Though Conrad is frequently (and justly) compared to James, from one angle there is no important modern novelist who less resembles him. For Conrad's complex narrative strategies examine not nuances of gesture, nor even, essentially, moral subtleties—even Marlow, after all, admits that Jim's case is "simple"—but crucial problems of conduct. These problems are profoundly moral and psychological, of course, but if they threaten psychic disintegration, the urgency with which they do so is a consequence primarily of the fact that these dilemmas of conduct also promise literal annihilation. The illusion, the mistake, even (most frighteningly) the mischance of calm or storm over which man has no control—these things can not only maim or undermine a man's sense of himself and his commitments in life, they can, quite simply, kill him. The threat of death or disintegration in Conrad's fiction is nearly always double: it is both spiritual or moral or psychological *and* at the same time palpably physical, something you feel on your pulses, something that happens *out there,* and happens to others outside yourself to whom you are bound by the ties of community:

> When the time came the blackness would overwhelm silently the bit of starlight falling upon the ship, and the end of all things would come without a sigh, stir, or murmur of any kind, and all our hearts would cease to beat like run-down clocks.
>
> It was impossible to shake off that sense of finality. The quietness that came over me was like a foretaste of annihilation.[17]

I take this passage to be representative of the double appeal of Conrad's finest work, which is modern and Romantic simultaneously. The spiritual, the interior testing mirrors the pressing physical ordeal that precedes and triggers it. And in what he himself would call this "purposely mingled resonance"—in this balance between the claims of external disaster and of psychic collapse, between the deed and the words that describe and evaluate the deed—we must see, I think, Conrad's lonely distinction.

Notes

PREFACE

1   In the preface to *The Nigger of the "Narcissus,"* pp. x–xi.

2   Letter of August 28, 1908. *Letters from Joseph Conrad, 1895–1924,* ed. Edward Garnett (1928; rpt. New York, 1962), p. 214.

3   See, for example, Eloise Knapp Hay, *The Political Novels of Joseph Conrad* (Chicago, 1963) and Avrom Fleishman, *Conrad's Politics* (Baltimore, 1967).

4   Leo Gurko, *Joseph Conrad: Giant in Exile* (New York, 1962).

5   Claire Rosenfield, *Paradise of Snakes: An Archetypal Analysis of Conrad's Political Novels* (Chicago, 1967). The quoted phrase is the title of Rosenfield's fifth chapter.

6   J. Hillis Miller, *Poets of Reality* (Cambridge, Mass., 1965), p. 1. Miller has elaborated his account of Conrad's nihilistic side in a recent essay, "The Interpretation of *Lord Jim,*" in *The Interpretation of Narrative,* ed. Morton W. Bloomfield, Harvard English Studies, no. 1 (Cambridge, Mass., 1970), pp. 211–28; and his influence is pervasive in Royal Roussel's *The Metaphysics of Darkness: A Study in the Unity and Development of Conrad's Fiction* (Baltimore, 1971). Conrad's existential qualities are treated in Edward Said's impressive *Joseph Conrad and the Fiction of Autobiography* (Cambridge, Mass., 1966) and in Bruce Johnson's *Conrad's Models of Mind* (Minneapolis, 1971). Though the two books last cited describe a Conrad more modern than Romantic, neither is wholly in conflict with the Conrad I will invoke. Johnson's emphasis on parallels between Conrad and Schopenhauer and his discussion of language in *Heart of Darkness,* and Said's extended commentary on *The Shadow-Line* are, in different ways, congruent with my argument.

7   See, for example, René Wellek, "Romanticism Re-examined," in *Concepts of Criticism* (New Haven, 1963), p. 218.

8   Thomas Moser, *Joseph Conrad: Achievement and Decline* (Cambridge, Mass., 1957).

CHAPTER 1

1   Quoted in Richard Curle, *The Last Twelve Years of Joseph Conrad* (London, 1928), p. 41.

2   Letter of July 17, 1923. *Conrad to a Friend: 150 Selected Letters from Joseph Conrad to Richard Curle,* ed. Richard Curle (London, 1928), p. 194.

3   *The Last Twelve Years of Joseph Conrad,* p. 195.

4   F. R. Leavis, "Joseph Conrad," *Sewanee Review,* 66 (1958), 183. Evidence of the ill-temper mentioned in the next sentence will be found in this same essay, pp. 184–86.

5   *Spectator,* 75 (1895), 530. This review is, in fact, quite intelligent within certain limits: *Almayer's Folly* is praised as "a decidedly powerful story of an uncommon type" which "breaks new ground in fiction."

6   Vernon Young, "Trial by Water: Joseph Conrad's *The Nigger of the 'Narcissus,'*" in *The Art of Joseph Conrad: A Critical Symposium,* ed. R. W. Stallman (East Lansing, Mich., 1960), pp. 109, 119. This essay appeared originally in *Accent,* 12 (1952), 67–81. Ian Watt supplies the answers to my rhetorical questions in his crucial essay, "Conrad Criticism and *The Nigger of the 'Narcissus,'*" *Nineteenth-Century Fiction,* 12 (1958), 257–83.

7   Gurko, *Joseph Conrad: Giant in Exile,* p. 72.

8   James Payne, "Our Note Book," *Illustrated London News,* 112 (1898), 172.

9   Curle, *Conrad to a Friend,* p. 188.

10   *Athenaeum,* May 2, 1903, pp. 558–59.

11   *Academy,* May 9, 1903, p. 463. I suspect this unsigned article is by Garnett, who had reviewed *Youth* in the *Academy* in the previous year (Dec. 6, 1902, pp. 606–07). Even the impatience with Conrad's method suggested in the passage quoted is not evidence of the critic's obtuseness and may merely be a concession to the plain tastes of potential readers. Later in the essay there is this acute sentence concerning Conrad's narrative manner: "For this indirectness, this returning upon himself, this effect, often disconcerting, of an abruptly introduced outside com-

ment, are inherent parts of the extraordinary subjectivity of Mr. Conrad's method."

12 See, for example, *Bookman* (London), 24 (1903), 108–09 (signed by A. T. Quiller-Couch); *Athenaeum,* Dec. 20, 1902, p. 824; *Spectator* (an illuminating sequence, showing Conrad's growing reputation) 81 (1898), 219; 85 (1900), 753; 89 (1902), 827–28 (signed by Hugh Clifford); 90 (1903), 823.

13 *Saturday Review* (London), 79 (1895), 797.

14 Garnett, *Letters from Conrad,* p. 53. For Conrad's ambivalent response to the Wells review see this letter; also a letter to his publisher quoted in Jocelyn Baines, *Joseph Conrad: A Critical Biography* (London, 1960), pp. 166–67; and finally his letter to Wells in *Joseph Conrad: Life and Letters,* 2 vols., ed. G. Jean-Aubry (London and New York, 1927), 1 : 248.

15 *Saturday Review* (London), 81 (1896), 509–10.

16 *Athenaeum,* Nov. 3, 1900, p. 576.

17 *National Observer,* 15 (1896), 680. It is possible that the *Observer*'s review of *Almayer's Folly* was written by the same hand, for the earlier article complains that Conrad had spoiled his "fresh and unconventional" material by a "laboured and muddleheaded involution. The sequence of events is at times very hard to follow, and now and then the reader becomes bored and bewildered" (14 [1895], 513).

18 *Sketch,* 11 (1895), 314.

19 Consider, as but one example, the opening sentences of Jerome Thale's widely known article on *Heart of Darkness:* "Conrad's 'Heart of Darkness' has all the trappings of the conventional adventure story—mystery, exotic setting, escape, suspense, unexpected attack. These, of course, are only the vehicle of something more fundamental, and one way of getting at what they symbolize is to see the story as a grail quest" ("Marlowe's [*sic*] Quest," in *Joseph Conrad's "Heart of Darkness": Backgrounds and Criticism,* ed. Leonard F. Dean [Englewood Cliffs, N.J., 1960], p. 159). This essay was first published in the *University of Toronto Quarterly,* 24 (1955), 351–58.

20 Both quotations in this paragraph are drawn from Curle, *The Last Twelve Years of Joseph Conrad,* p. 166.

21 Curle, *Conrad to a Friend,* p. 190.

22 Tom Hopkinson, "The Short Stories," in "Joseph Conrad: A Critical Symposium," *London Magazine*, 4 (1957), 38–39.
23 Albert Guerard, *Conrad the Novelist* (Cambridge, Mass., 1958), pp. 67–68.
24 Morton Zabel, *Craft and Character in Modern Fiction* (New York, 1957), p. 170.
25 *Joseph Conrad: Letters to William Blackwood and David S. Meldrum,* ed. William Blackburn (Durham, N.C., 1958), p. 156.
26 Zdzislaw Najder, ed., *Conrad's Polish Background* (London, 1964), p. 211.
27 Ibid., pp. 2–3. Najder says that the term *szlachta* "cannot be adequately rendered in English because there was no difference in Poland between nobility and gentry: every member of the *szlachta* was legally equal to any other member, however rich; . . . any member of the *szlachta* could theoretically become a member of the . . . Polish parliament . . . or even be elected a king" (p. 2, n. 2).
28 Jean-Aubry, *Conrad: Life and Letters,* 1 : 41.
29 See Baines's *Conrad: A Critical Biography,* pp. 33–59, for a thorough and persuasive discussion of the evidence.
30 "Geography and Some Explorers," *Last Essays,* pp. 16–17. Conrad repeats the story in *A Personal Record* (p. 13), and uses it in *Heart of Darkness* (p. 52) where Marlow tells the anecdote of himself.
31 Letter of April 23, 1893. H. V. Marrot, *The Life and Letters of John Galsworthy* (London, 1935), p. 88.
32 It seems unnecessary to cite particular letters. The letters to Garnett and Meldrum are in volumes previously cited; those to Marguerite Poradowska in *Letters of Joseph Conrad to Marguerite Poradowska,* trans. and ed. John A. Gee and Paul J. Sturm (New Haven, 1940).
33 The first quotation is from Ford's *Joseph Conrad: A Personal Remembrance* (London, 1924), p. 25; the second is from his *Return to Yesterday* (London, 1931), p. 24.
34 Wells's account of Conrad is given in the second volume of his *Experiment in Autobiography,* 2 vols. (London, 1934). All my quotations are drawn from pp. 615–22.
35 Baines, *Conrad: A Critical Biography,* p. 234.
36 Ibid., p. 50.

37   The letters to Colvin are in Jean-Aubry, *Conrad: Life and
     Letters,* 2 : 224, 229; the inscription is accessible in *Notes
     by Joseph Conrad Written in a Set of His First Editions
     . . .* , ed. Richard Curle (London, 1925), p. 33.
38   Curle, *The Last Twelve Years of Joseph Conrad,* pp. 11,
     21, 42, 31.
39   Garnett, *Letters from Conrad,* Introduction, p. 12.
40   Zabel, *Craft and Character in Modern Fiction,* p. 167.

<h3 style="text-align:center">CHAPTER 2</h3>

1   Lawrence Graver believes that the enormous popular suc-
     cess of *The Prisoner of Zenda* not only helped to create a
     market for exotic romances during the nineties but also
     may have helped to set the tone for the kind of material
     published in the *Pall Mall Magazine* (*Conrad's Short
     Fiction* [Berkeley and Los Angeles, 1969], pp. 92–93).
     This journal was to publish a fair amount of Conrad's
     work, including *Typhoon* and five chapters from *The
     Mirror of the Sea.* On Conrad's relations with the *Pall
     Mall* see below, pp. 184–86, n. 14.
2   George Sampson, *The Concise Cambridge History of
     English Literature,* 2d ed. (1961), p. 798.
3   Edward Garnett, trying to assure the author of *Almayer's
     Folly* that if he committed himself to writing as a career
     he would not have to live in an attic, mentioned Steven-
     son, Kipling, and Haggard as examples of "public favor-
     ites." Garnett recalled that Conrad thought Haggard "too
     horrible for words" (*Letters from Conrad,* Introduction,
     p. 9).
4   A. T. Quiller-Couch, "Robert Louis Stevenson," in *Ad-
     ventures in Criticism* (London, 1896), p. 184. This essay
     originally appeared in the *Speaker,* Dec. 22, 1894.
5   Joseph Jacobs in the *Athenaeum,* quoted by Robert
     Kiely, *Robert Louis Stevenson and the Fiction of Adven-
     ture* (Cambridge, Mass., 1964), p. 7.
6   This is notably true of *The Master of Ballantrae* (1889);
     The Ebb-Tide (1894), a dark fable of human weakness
     written in collaboration with Lloyd Osbourne that has
     not received its due even from Stevenson's recent sympa-
     thetic critics; and the unfinished *Weir of Hermiston,*
     published posthumously in 1896.

There are illuminating references to Conrad in Kiely's book, cited in the previous note, and in Edwin M. Eigner's *Robert Louis Stevenson and Romantic Tradition* (Princeton, 1966). Both see Stevenson in some degree as Conrad's precursor.

7   Conrad was disappointed in his hopes for a financial success with *Romance*. Things looked promising at first, though. In November 1903, Conrad wrote Galsworthy that the book had gone into a second printing just one month after its publication, and observed wryly: "That is better than anything of mine has ever done. *Et voilà!* What a Romance!" (Jean-Aubry, *Conrad: Life and Letters*, 1 : 322).

8   To Kasimierz Waliszewski, the historian and literary man who was preparing an article on Conrad's work; Nov. 8, 1903 (Najder, *Conrad's Polish Background*, p. 236).

9   Quoted by Baines, *Conrad: A Critical Biography*, p. 271.

10 Ford, *Conrad: A Personal Remembrance*, p. 28. Conrad's hope that the matter of the novel would have wide appeal was entirely reasonable even if it was finally disappointed. The public's passion for romances—a passion that surely influenced the collaborators in their choice of a title—had scarcely subsided by the turn of the century, as the advertisements for new books in the literary journals of the period abundantly demonstrate. In a typical page of ads for new offerings which ran in the *Athenaeum* (Sept. 26, 1903, p. 401) just prior to the appearance there of a review of *Romance,* a single London publishing house listed eleven works of fiction, eight of which promise in varying combinations the satisfactions of exotic local color, historical settings, and action-packed plots. One book in particular, *Padmini: An Indian Romance,* by T. Ramakrishna, appears to aim at every taste; the blurb reads: "A story of Southern India in the Seventeenth Century; portrays the overthrow of the great Vizianagar House by the usurper Saluva." Other titles in the list include *The Soul of Chivalry,* by an anonymous writer, and *Cristina: A Historical Romance of Mediaeval Italy,* by Emily Underdown.

    The *Athenaeum* carried its review of *Romance* six issues later (Nov. 7, p. 610). The review is friendly but

restrained, judging *Romance* a "fine story," "fittingly
named," but deciding firmly that it suffered in comparison with the "masterly and distinguished" books Conrad
had published on his own.

11 Foreword to *Five Letters by Joseph Conrad Written to
Edward Noble in 1895,* ed. Noble (London, 1925), p. 8.
There were other gestures toward collaboration in his
early writing years. In 1894, before *Almayer's Folly* had
been accepted for publication, Conrad suggested to Marguerite Poradowska that they publish a translation of the
novel "as a collaboration" (Gee and Sturm, *Letters of Joseph Conrad to Marguerite Poradowska,* p. 73). And in
1898 Conrad and Stephen Crane talked seriously about
collaborating on a play. Garnett (*Letters from Conrad,*
pp. 11–12) and Conrad himself (Jean-Aubry, *Conrad: Life
and Letters,* 1 : 228; "Stephen Crane," *Last Essays,* pp.
115–16) claim Conrad was not keen on the idea. But a
letter from Conrad to Crane clearly shows that he was in
fact rather excited by the possibility of working jointly
with the author of *The Red Badge of Courage:* "Your
idea is good—I am certain. Perhaps you, yourself, don't
know how good it is. I ask you as a . . . favour to let me
have a sketch of it . . . I would be only too glad to work
by your side and with your lead" ("The Letters of Joseph
Conrad to Stephen and Nora Crane," ed. Carl Bohnen-
berger and Norman M. Hill, *Bookman* (New York), 69
[May 1929], 232).

12 Both Frank MacShane (*The Life and Work of Ford
Madox Ford* [New York, 1965], pp. 36–38) and Baines
(*Conrad: A Critical Biography,* pp. 216–22) emphasize
Conrad's desire to gain fluency in writing English (a notion I find unpersuasive since by this time Conrad had already completed *The Nigger of the "Narcissus"*), his desperate   financial   circumstances,   and   his   general
unproductiveness. But neither suggests that Ford's subject
might have interested Conrad as literature.

13 Garnett, *Letters from Conrad,* p. 180.

14 The quoted phrase is Ford's (*Return to Yesterday,* p. 55).

15 Oct. 18, 1898. Quoted by Baines, *Conrad: A Critical Biography,* p. 217 (emphasis added). Baines believes Conrad is
referring here not to *Romance* but to *The Inheritors*

(1901), but this is extremely unlikely. See Arthur Mizener, *The Saddest Story: A Biography of Ford Madox Ford* (New York, 1971), p. 42.

16 Garnett, *Letters from Conrad*, p. 110.

17 Blackburn, *Conrad: Letters to Blackwood*, p. 154.

18 This excerpt is from a letter to James Pinker, Conrad's literary agent, dated Jan. 6, 1902 (quoted by Baines, *Conrad: A Critical Biography*, p. 275).

19 This cannot be said of *The Inheritors*, about which Conrad was never serious and which, according to Curle, he intended to eliminate from his collected edition (*The Last Twelve Years of Joseph Conrad*, pp. 111–12). As he wrote to Garnett: "What a lark! I set myself to look upon the thing as a sort of skit upon the sort of political (?!) novel, fools of the N.S. [*New Statesman?*] sort do write. . . . And poor H[ueffer] was dead in earnest! Oh Lord. How he worked!" (*Letters from Conrad*, p. 168).

20 Curle, *Notes by Joseph Conrad in a Set of His First Editions*, p. 23. Compare his laconic inscription in Thomas Wise's copy of *The Inheritors:* "The idea of this book is entirely Hueffer's, and so is most of the writing" (Thomas J. Wise, *A Conrad Library* [London, 1928], p. 6).

21 That Conrad may well have exaggerated his contribution to the novel in his inscription in Curle's copy is further evidence of his regard for *Romance*. In any event, in a letter to Ford recapitulating each man's part in the composition of the novel Conrad claims to have written about half the book and concludes: "Intellectually and artistically it is of course, right through, a joint production" (quoted by Baines, *Conrad: A Critical Biography*, p. 271). Ford quotes a portion of this same letter in his appendix to their third, and last, collaboration, *The Nature of a Crime* (collected edition, 1924, p. 95) and agrees with Conrad's account of the division of labor. Both *The Inheritors* and *The Nature of a Crime* have been dropped from the current collected edition of Conrad's works.

22 Author's note, *The Arrow of Gold*, p. ix. See also the author's notes to *Tales of Unrest*, p. vii; and the preface to *The Shorter Tales of Joseph Conrad*, reprinted in *Last Essays*, p. 145.

23 Ford, *Conrad: A Personal Remembrance,* p. 29.
24 It was not unusual for Conrad to visit the British Museum in order to do background reading for books he was working on or intended to write (Curle, *The Last Twelve Years,* p. 77). In a letter to Pinker in 1905 (Jean-Aubry, *Conrad: Life and Letters,* 2 : 13) Conrad gives an account of his discovery of a subject that is fairly typical of his way of working: "I've found here the subject of my Mediterranean novel. . . . It is the struggle for Capri in 1808 between the French and the English. I have access here to the collection of books and Ms. belonging to Dr. Cerio." Conrad frequently used books to refresh his memory and to provide background data. In a letter to Blackwood he speaks of the "dull, wise books" he turned to for details in his Malayan stories (Blackburn, *Conrad: Letters to Blackwood,* p. 34). In an unpublished letter to Ford—one in a particularly illuminating series of fifty-three letters to his collaborator written during the period 1898–1904 now in the possession of the Beinecke Library at Yale—Conrad asks: "Pray can you procure me a life of Garibaldi—a picturesque one? Didn't he write an Auto? I have a vague notion of something of the sort existing under the eyes of Dumas the father" (March 23, 1903).
25 Blackburn, *Conrad: Letters to Blackwood,* pp. 129–30.
26 "The Original Nostromo: Conrad's Source," *Review of English Studies,* n.s. 10 (1959), 52.
27 Beinecke Library, reprinted in George T. Keating, *A Conrad Memorial Library* (Garden City, N.Y., 1929), pp. 131–33.
28 Ford, *Conrad: A Personal Remembrance,* p. 204.
29 Keating, *A Conrad Memorial Library,* p. 131. I cite this volume rather than the original document because it is more accessible.
30 Ford makes the credible claim that it was during their work on *Romance* that he and Conrad discovered the principle of "*progression d'effet,* words for which there is no English equivalent"; the pair realized, Ford says, "that every word set on paper—*every* word set on paper—must carry the story forward faster and faster and with more and more intensity" (*Conrad: A Personal Remembrance,* p.

210). Though these remarks bear most importantly on books like *Lord Jim* or *The Good Soldier,* their application to *Romance* seems clear enough.

31   Beinecke Library, undated but written in the summer or fall of 1903.

32   There is no reason to doubt the at least partial truth of Conrad's statement to Kazimierz Waliszewski (in the letter cited above, n. 8) that he collaborated on *Romance* "at a time when it was impossible for me to do anything else."

33   Quoted by Baines, *Conrad: A Critical Biography,* p. 217.

34   There are also several interesting parallels between *Treasure Island* and *Romance*. These are sensibly discussed in Richard J. Herndon, "The Collaboration of Joseph Conrad with Ford Madox Ford" (Ph.D. diss., Stanford University, 1957), pp. 212–14.

35   In an unpublished letter effusively complimenting Ford on the publication of *The Fifth Queen Crowned* (1908), Conrad wrote: "Any prose read directly after yours produce[s] the effect of thick mouthing. That anybody could mention, in connection with you, that Virtuoso Cymballist Stevenson passes my comprehension" (Beinecke Library, Feb. 20, 1908). Conrad's low opinion of Stevenson's prose style is implied, too, in these revealing lines from a letter to Alfred Knopf: "When it comes to popularity I stand much nearer the public mind than Stevenson, who was super-literary, a conscious virtuoso of style; whereas the average mind does not care much for virtuosity" (July 20, 1913; Jean-Aubry, *Conrad: Life and Letters,* 2: 147). According to Curle, Conrad "always spoke, apart from his book on the South Seas, with aversion of Stevenson, whom he regarded as an artist of small account" (*The Last Twelve Years,* p. 117). The book of which Conrad approved was not fiction but a collection of travel pieces.

36   Yet, curiously, the chief villain of *Romance,* O'Brien, has a pirate namesake in chapters 25 and 26 of *Treasure Island.* And it may also be significant that Sebright, the ship's mate in *Romance,* bears the same name as a ship's officer who appears in chapter 17 of the R.L.S.–Lloyd Osbourne collaboration, *The Wrecker.* This last coincidence is tantalizing because we know W. E. Henley invoked this

famous partnership in his letter to Conrad about the plan
to work with Ford and because Sebright is one of the very
few characters Conrad invented himself (Curle, *Notes by
Joseph Conrad,* p. 23).

37 *The Master of Ballantrae, Works,* Thistle Edition (New
York, 1902), 9 : i.

38 Author's note, *The Shadow-Line,* p. vii. He says the same
thing implicitly in the author's note to *Almayer's Folly,*
pp. vii–viii. But his most forceful statement on the subject is in two letters to Richard Curle written in July 1923
(*Conrad to a Friend,* pp. 188–96).

39 The fragment—that is how Conrad himself describes it in
his preface—is *The Nature of a Crime.* The quotation is
from Ford, *Conrad: A Personal Remembrance,* pp. 46, 47.
In the appendix to *The Nature of a Crime* Ford repeats
the same notion, remarking that their collaboration on
Romance "was the continual attempt on the part of the
one collaborator to key up and of the other to key
down" (pp. 96–97).

40 Jean-Aubry, *Conrad: Life and Letters,* 1 : 312.

41 MacShane, *The Life and Work of Ford Madox Ford,* p.
49.

42 *TLS,* Oct. 30, 1903, p. 312.

43 The first two passages are from the fourth part of the
book and are therefore almost certainly Conrad's; according to Ford, "the matchless Fourth Part is both in conception and writing entirely the work of Mr. Conrad" (Appendix, *The Nature of a Crime,* p. 95). The third
quotation is the novel's final paragraph and is by Ford.
But Conrad is equally responsible for this passage because
he worked very closely with Ford on the book's final
pages. See his letter to Ford (Jean-Aubry, *Conrad: Life
and Letters,* 1: 318–19) where he goes into detail about an
earlier version of the ending and where he speaks of lines
that remain in the published text.

It is perhaps worth noting that the published text of
Romance is in general less pretentious than the portions
of the manuscript I have been able to examine. Despite
changes that are only partially successful, and despite
other, rarer alterations that seem to make the tone more
pretentious than before, the tendency of the revisions is to

eliminate or minimize the verbal extravagance of the manuscript. Though the following passage from the novel is scarcely a tribute to Conrad's artistry, it is considerably less grandiloquent than the same passage from the manuscript:

> I suffered from the lucidity of my feelings. I saw, with indignation, my own wretched self being angled for like a fish. And with all that, in my forlorn state, I remained prudent. I did not rush out blindly. No. I approached the inner end of the passage, as though I had been stalking a wild creature, slowly, from the side. I crept along the wall of the cavern, and protruded my head far enough to look at the fiendish temptation. [p. 409]

Here is the manuscript version:

> I suffered from a horrible lucidity; a man between love and—not death—but the difficulty to live: torn between the most idealised of human passions and the brutal need to quench an intolerable thirst. And this necessity of my tormented body was bound with the very welfare of my soul on earth whatever mercy it might have expected beyond. I was sane enough to see with indignation my own wretched self being angled for like a fish. And with all that, in my forlorn state, I remained prudent. I did not rush out blindly. No. I approached the inner end of the passage as though I had been stalking a wild creature slowly, from the side; creeping along the wall of the cavern; intending to protrude my head far enough to look at the bait. [MS, pp. 464–65]

The differences here between the published version and the manuscript are fairly representative, and we can only regret that Conrad and Ford did not pursue the work of revision with greater rigor. (The passage from the novel quoted above is from the collected edition. It is identical in wording to the same passage in the first English edition and in the first American edition.)

The manuscript fragment to which I refer here is in

the Beinecke Library at Yale. Entirely in Conrad's hand, the manuscript comprises 184 pages, which fall into two nonsequential parts corresponding to pp. 142–71 and pp. 402–43 of the text as published in the collected edition. My examination of this manuscript further confirms the extent of Conrad's serious commitment to *Romance,* for a fair number of pages in the manuscript have been very painstakingly worked and reworked by Conrad.

44 See Thomas Moser's chapter, "The Uncongenial Subject," in *Joseph Conrad: Achievement and Decline,* pp. 50–130. "The failure of the lover's masculinity," Moser summarizes, is the "implicit subject of the later novels" (p. 129).

45 In *Return to Yesterday* (p. 25) Ford explains how he came to write one of the novel's magazine installments, and his claim is substantiated by the existence of sixteen pages of the *Nostromo* manuscript in Ford's hand (Beinecke Library). These pages, numbered 588–603, correspond to pp. 175–85 of the collected edition *Nostromo.* It appears certain that the fragment does not represent Ford's entire contribution to the novel since it breaks off in mid-sentence. When the existence of this manuscript became known it was first suggested that Ford had written the passage down from Conrad's dictation (see, for example, Baines, *Conrad: A Critical Biography,* p. 292). But Mizener's authoritative account finally vindicated Ford (see *The Saddest Story,* pp. 89–91).

Only a few months after beginning *Nostromo,* Conrad wrote Ford about his new book: "I do not doubt of your assistance in my efforts. You must run down and see me soon" (March 23, 1903; Beinecke Library). And in August of the same year Conrad wrote to Pinker: "If people want to begin printing (serial) say in Sept^{er} you may let them safely—for you know that, at the very worst, H [uef-fer] stands in the background (quite confidentially you understand)." This excerpt is from a letter printed in *Life and Letters* (1: 315–16). But Jean-Aubry has tampered with it, substituting *M* for *H* without indicating his intervention. Baines (pp. 291–92) corrects the error in his quotation from the original document.

46 Frederick R. Karl, *A Reader's Guide to Joseph Conrad* (New York, 1960), p. 152. For another useful account of

Romance's place in Conrad's oeuvre, see Ivo Vidan, "Rehearsal for 'Nostromo,'" *Studia Romanica et Anglica Zagrabiensia,* no. 12 (1961), pp. 9–16.

47 Karl, *A Reader's Guide to Joseph Conrad,* pp. 149–50.

48 Surely Baines is wrong when he says that "in conception and spirit the book owes little to Conrad. The subject was originally Hueffer's and it is easy to see why the romantic adventures of the aristocratic young John Kemp would have appealed to him" (*Conrad: A Critical Biography,* p. 275). I would argue, in fact, that the reverse is true: it is easy to see why the substance of *Romance* would appeal to Conrad, but less easy to understand why it should have interested the author of *The Good Soldier* or *Parade's End.* Even if one concedes the resemblances between *Romance* and Ford's historical novels, the fact remains that his lasting achievements as a novelist lie elsewhere, while Conrad's serious fiction has profound affinities with *Romance.*

49 Kiely, *Robert Louis Stevenson and the Fiction of Adventure,* p. 20.

50 Marvin Mudrick, ed., *Conrad: A Collection of Critical Essays* (Englewood Cliffs, N.J., 1966), Introduction, p. 10. This iconoclastic essay brilliantly challenges the prevailing critical estimate of Conrad, judging the early novellas to be the only true source of Conrad's distinction.

51 Moser, *Joseph Conrad: Achievement and Decline,* p. 180.

52 Ibid., p. 193.

53 Robert Louis Stevenson, "Pastoral," *Memories and Portraits, Works* (New York, 1902), 13 : 238.

54 Norman Sherry, *Conrad's Eastern World* (Cambridge, 1966); *Conrad's Western World* (Cambridge, 1971). John Gordan, *Joseph Conrad: The Making of a Novelist* (Cambridge, Mass., 1940). The map is provided in *Conrad's Eastern World,* p. 177.

55 In the prefaces cited above, n. 22.

56 Morton Zabel, ed., *The Portable Conrad* (New York, 1947), Introduction, p. 41.

57 Zabel, *Craft and Character in Modern Fiction,* p. 172.

58 Jean-Aubry, *Conrad: Life and Letters,* 1 : 283.

CHAPTER 3

1   See Baines, *Conrad: A Critical Biography,* p. 354; and Gurko, *Joseph Conrad: Giant in Exile,* pp. 156–58.
2   Jean-Aubry, *Conrad: Life and Letters,* 2 : 87.
3   Guerard, *Conrad the Novelist,* p. 3.
4   It would be unjust to one of Conrad's most memorable passages to leave off with this brief remark. The fifteen pages devoted to the real-life Almayer are a major triumph in which Conrad exploits to the fullest the advantages of his reminiscential form. The whole section illustrates how brilliantly the material of *Almayer's Folly,* itself only rarely an effective book, would have been handled by the mature Conrad who had discovered his essential voice and technical gifts. A kind of anthology of many of the things we value in the author of *Lord Jim,* the episode is remarkable not only for its vivid rendering of the jungle landscape. At several points Conrad is entirely metamorphosed into a speculative narrator, a brother to Marlow, who supports his conjectures about the motives of his subject by citing evidence in breathless sentences whose very shape and accent reveal an urgency that hints at obsession. Here is one example:

> What he [Almayer] wanted with a pony goodness only knows, since I am perfectly certain he could not ride it; but here you have the man, ambitious, aiming at the grandiose, importing a pony, whereas in the whole settlement at which he used to shake daily his impotent fist, there was only one path that was practicable for a pony: a quarter of a mile at most, hedged in by hundreds of square leagues of virgin forest. But who knows? The importation of that Bali pony might have been part of some deep scheme. [p. 76]

The brilliant conclusion of the episode, a daring rhetorical maneuver in which Conrad defends his treatment of Almayer against the protests of that discontented man's imagined ghost, is particularly important for Vernon Young, who discovers there "the key to Conrad's interest in character." See his good essay, "Lingard's Folly: The Lost Subject," *Kenyon Review,* 15 (1953), 522–39.

5   In this unwritten version Razumov was to fall in love with Miss Haldin, to marry her, and in the end to confess that he had betrayed her brother; the confession was to be "brought about mainly by the resemblance of their child to the late Haldin" (Jean-Aubry, *Conrad: Life and Letters,* 2: 64–65).

6   Morton Zabel, ed., *Tales of Heroes and History* (New York, 1960), Introduction, pp. xii–xiii.

7   Though allusions to the departure from Poland occur elsewhere, the matter becomes most explicit in three passages: pp. 35–43, 110, 120–22. Most recent writers on Conrad have assumed that his defensive tone in these moments is a response to the charges of desertion brought publicly against him in 1899 by a Polish novelist. The best accounts of this attack on Conrad's patriotism—it was published in *Kraj,* a Polish weekly—and of the evidence for Conrad's awareness of it, are in Baines, *Conrad: A Critical Biography,* pp. 352–54; in Zdzislaw Najder, ed., *Conrad's Polish Background,* pp. 22–23; and in Eloise Knapp Hay, *The Political Novels of Joseph Conrad,* pp. 56–70.

8   That Jim is trapped in his son's need for a father's approval explains not only the rich ambiguity of his final act of self-sacrifice on Patusan but also the nature of his connections to Marlow, to Stein, even to the ship chandlers for whom he works as a water clerk. A number of critics have noticed the ironic parallel between the early incident of the training ship—in which Jim fails to jump into a longboat bound on a mission of rescue—and his later leap into the lifeboat when he deserts the *Patna.* The parallel is fully clarified when one realizes that in the first instance Jim's senior officer is beside him on deck, and to jump would be to desert the figure of authority; while in the second instance his captain is situated below, in the lifeboat, and beckons Jim to leave the ship. These and other arguments for Conrad's preoccupation with the relations of fathers and sons are placed in a psychoanalytic context in Robert M. Armstrong's "Joseph Conrad: The Conflict of Command," in *The Psychoanalytic Study*

of the Child, vol. 26, ed. Anna Freud et al. (New York, 1971), pp. 485–534.

9   This anonymous reviewer cares "least of all" for the Nelson postscript and "would have preferred to lay [the book] aside with the picture of the retreating Dominic in our eyes" (*TLS,* Oct. 12, 1906, p. 344). Misgivings of any sort were very rare in the reviews. For the writer, also anonymous, in the *Spectator* the badly overwritten chapters on the winds and the sea "reach[ed] at times a poetry which is almost sublime," while the concluding section was "one of the finest panegyrics of Nelson that we have read" (*Spectator,* 97 [1906], 889). The reviews of *The Mirror* strongly support John Gordan's conclusion, based on a study of the reviews of Conrad's earlier books, that the critics' "insistence on his inevitable unpopularity must have done him far more harm than all the inimical reviews put together" (*Joseph Conrad: The Making of a Novelist,* p. 303). The *Spectator* review just cited fairly represents the position of the other notices I have examined; in the midst of high praises, the review predicts poor sales: *The Mirror of the Sea* "is not a book for which we can foretell a ready sale. It is too subtle, too profound, too exacting in its appeal to take the fancy of the casual reader" (p. 889).

10 These two essays, the earliest to be published, appeared in the *Daily Mail* on March 8, November 16, and December 2, 1904. Baines has seen two letters to Pinker which indicate that "Conrad had originally thought of these articles as separate from the *Mirror* papers" (*Conrad: A Critical Biography,* p. 292). Of the fifteen titled sections in *The Mirror of the Sea,* thirteen appeared first, often under different titles, in periodicals. Chapter 10, "The Faithful River" (pp. 100–15), is the only other section to have been published in 1904. Except for "Initiation," which was published in 1906, and except for the two chapters which were never separately published, all the other chapters appeared as articles in 1905. In my remarks on the dating of sections, I follow Baines's careful bibliography (pp. 452–59) and Kenneth A. Lohf and Eugene P. Sheehy, *Joseph Conrad at Midcentury: Editions and Studies* (Minneapolis, 1957).

11   Jean-Aubry, *Conrad: Life and Letters,* 1 : 326–27.

12   Jean-Aubry, no friend to Ford, admits that Conrad dic-
      tated portions of the book to him (*The Sea Dreamer,*
      trans. Helen Sebba [New York, 1957], p. 244); and even
      Jessie Conrad, who deeply disliked Ford, admits that the
      book would not have been written without Ford's help
      (*Joseph Conrad and His Circle* [London, 1935], p. 87).
      But the tradition of denigrating Ford led even Jocelyn
      Baines to misread the evidence. See Mizener, *The Saddest
      Story,* pp. 88–89.

13   Ford, of course, played a crucial role as well in encourag-
      ing Conrad to write *A Personal Record.* There is no
      doubt that the later memoir would never have been writ-
      ten had not Ford helped Conrad by serving as his aman-
      uensis and by publishing installments of the book in the
      English Review, for whose pages the reminiscences were
      intended. See Baines, *Conrad: A Critical Biography,* pp.
      348–51; and also the marvelous Ford letter, inaccurate in
      minor details but surely exactly right in spirit, describing
      how he "coerced" his collaborator into working on the
      memoirs (*Letters of Ford Madox Ford,* ed. Richard M.
      Ludwig [Princeton, 1965], pp. 267–68).
         The more closely I compare their correspondence with
      what Ford says in his various memoirs about his work
      with Conrad, the more convinced I become of Ford's es-
      sential honesty. This conviction is especially the result of
      a very close reading of the Beinecke Library's extensive
      collection of materials relating to Ford and to Conrad,
      and particularly the sequence of fifty-three unpublished
      holograph letters from Conrad to Ford to which I have
      referred in previous notes. Baines, who apparently had ac-
      cess to these letters prior to their acquisition by Yale,
      makes very good use of selected passages from them, and
      Mizener draws upon them extensively as well. But a sys-
      tematic reading of the entire series clarifies aspects of the
      relationship between the two writers that have been
      slighted or distorted by everyone I have read. A full ac-
      count of Ford's immense—and immensely generous—
      contribution to Conrad's life and work still needs to be
      written.

14   May 29, 1904; Beinecke Library. Four months later Con-

rad sent Ford's wife Elsie a short note, enclosing a check "for Ford's proportion of [*The Mirror*] Sketches" (Sept. 19, 1904; Beinecke Library).

Conrad's hopes for a favorable response from Harvey were at least partially gratified, for two chapters of the book first appeared in *Harper's Weekly,* though apparently its editor either refused to bid on the six sketches the *Pall Mall Magazine* had offered to accept or failed to match the *Pall Mall*'s price. In any event, Conrad's claim that Harvey was prepared to accept the sketches in book form is borne out by the fact that the firm of Harper and Brothers, of which Harvey was then president, published the American edition of *The Mirror of the Sea* in 1906, the year of its English publication by Methuen.

Col. George Brinton McClellan Harvey (1864–1928) was also at this time editor and owner of the *North American Review.* It is very likely that the negotiations over the sea sketches began Conrad's profitable association with Harvey. Not only did this editor publish two of the sea sketches in *Harper's Weekly* and arrange for the publication of the American edition of *The Mirror,* but he also appears to have grabbed Conrad for the *North American Review.* In 1905, the same year in which the sea sketches appeared in *Harper's Weekly,* Conrad published in the *North American Review* two of the essays ("Autocracy and War" and "Henry James") that he later collected in *Notes on Life and Letters.* Five years later, Conrad serialized *Under Western Eyes* in the *North American Review* (Dec. 1910–Oct. 1911).

This letter to Ford has additional importance because it tells us something about Conrad's opinion of the *Pall Mall Magazine:* he feels his work will be "thrown away" if it is published there. Yet in 1902 he published both *Typhoon* and "Tomorrow" in its pages, and after the sea sketches he was to give more of his fiction to the magazine: "Gaspar Ruiz" in 1906, "The Duel" in 1908, and "The Inn of the Two Witches" in 1913. It is significant, as Lawrence Graver has written, that these stories are among Conrad's "most optimistic and least demanding works" (*Conrad's Short Fiction* [Berkeley and Los Angeles, 1969], p. 94). Graver's discussion of the middlebrow orientation of the *Pall Mall* accords with my own conclusions, based on an examination of several years' worth of material published during the time Conrad was writing for the magazine.

15   Lavishly illustrated, the articles ran under the general title *The Mirror of the Sea.* The chapter headings in the magazine version were retained for the book, with the exception of "Emblems of Hope," which had been "Up Anchor" in the *Pall Mall* version (*Pall Mall Magazine*, 35 [1905], 104–09, 183–88, 363–68, 439–46, 580–87, 718–23).

16   Baines, *Conrad: A Critical Biography*, pp. 290–91. Baines's excerpt eliminates a long clause without indicating its excision and creates paragraph divisions where none exist. It is possible that he was quoting from a copy of the letter rather than the original.

17   The first five chapters of *The Mirror,* plus the two articles for the *Daily Mail* that were later incorporated into the book (see n. 9 above), were all "written while the Conrads were . . . in London" during March 1904, living near Ford and his family, and sharing household expenses and meals with them (Baines, p. 292). Since later in March Conrad returned to the Pent with his family while Ford remained in London, it is possible that their separation brought an end to their plans to write *The Mirror* jointly. But it is also possible that Conrad never intended to collaborate on the book and merely spoke of collaboration in the beginning in order to take advantage of Ford's willingness to help him. In a letter to Col. Harvey more than a month prior to his letter to Ford ending the collaboration, Conrad described his plans for "a volume of sea sketches, something in the spirit of Turgeniev's *Sportsman's Sketches,* but concerned with ships and the sea with a distinct autobiographical and anecdotal note running through what is mainly meant for a record of remembered feelings" (April 15, 1904, quoted by Baines, p. 326). From this excerpt it is clear that Conrad made no suggestion in his letter to the American publisher that the book was to be a collaboration.

18   I have closely compared the articles which appeared in the *Pall Mall* with the published book. There are a few

occasions when Conrad adds whole paragraphs to the book in an effort to make the transitions between sections more coherent. But usually his alterations are minor enough to permit him to retain the paragraph divisions of the magazine version. Still, he revised with care, for although his changes in wording rarely compel him to alter the original syntax significantly, he makes numerous, and often very minute, substantive changes. I quote here a fairly representative example. The second passage, which I take to be an improvement, is from the collected edition, whose wording is identical with that of the first English and the 1921 Heinemann's collected edition. The first American edition retains the phrase *at sea* from the last sentence of the magazine version, but in other respects is identical in wording to the other editions. I have italicized the substantive changes from the magazine version.

> No!—the seaman of three hundred years hence will probably be neither touched nor moved to derision, affection, or admiration. He will look upon the photogravures of our nearly defunct sailing-ships with a cold, inquisitive, but indifferent eye. Our ships of yesterday will be to his ships no ancestors, but predecessors. Their course will have been run and their race extinct. Whatever craft he handles at sea, he will be not our descendant, but our successor. [*Pall Mall Magazine*, 35 (1905), 364]

> No; the *seamen* of three hundred years hence will probably be neither touched nor moved to derision, affection, or admiration. *They* will *glance at* the photogravures of our nearly defunct sailing-ships with a cold, inquisitive, *and* indifferent eye. Our ships of yesterday will *stand* to *their* ships *as* no *lineal* ancestors, but *as mere* predecessors *whose* course will have been run and *the* race extinct. Whatever craft he handles *with skill, the seaman of the future shall* be not our descendant, but *only* our successor. [*Mirror*, pp. 72–73]

19 Morton Zabel, ed., *The Shadow-Line and Two Other Tales* (New York, 1959), Introduction, p. 13.

20 See Watt's "Conrad Criticism and *The Nigger of the 'Narcissus,'*" *Nineteenth-Century Fiction,* 12 (1958), 257–83, esp. 263–66.

21 Leavis, "Joseph Conrad," *Sewanee Review,* 66 (1958), 189; Irving Howe, *Politics and the Novel* (New York, 1957), p. 81.

22 Blackburn, *Conrad: Letters to Blackwood,* p. 138.

23 F. R. Leavis, *The Great Tradition* (1948; rpt. New York, 1954), p. 230.

24 The episode first appeared as an independent whole in *Blackwood's Magazine* (Jan. 1906). "Maga"'s editors apparently regarded it as fiction, for it was reprinted in one of the firm's story collections. See *'Blackwood' Tales from the Outposts: VI, Tales of the Sea* (Edinburgh and London, 1933).

25 Watt, "Conrad Criticism and *The Nigger of the 'Narcissus,'*" pp. 281–82.

26 That lament is, of course, most significantly embodied in *The Nigger of the 'Narcissus,'* and Conrad's references to the subject in *The Mirror,* their own considerable independent value aside, are a useful gloss on the novel. Those references also clarify this somewhat cryptic incomplete sentence from *The Shadow-Line:* "For no reason on which a sensible person could put a finger I threw up my job—chucked my berth—left the ship of which the worst that could be said was that she was a steamship and therefore, perhaps, not entitled to that blind loyalty which . . ." (p. 4; ellipsis Conrad's).

27 It is essential to point out that my analysis of the *Tremolino* episode completely ignores the tangled biographical problems it poses. Since my emphasis is on the literary qualities of the episode, on what it reveals of Conrad's imagination of the world, its apparent unreliability as autobiography is, for my purposes, peripheral. Still, Conrad's accounts of the *Tremolino* incident and of the whole of his experiences in Marseilles as a young man (in *The Mirror, The Arrow of Gold,* and elsewhere) depart so drastically from the facts Jocelyn Baines has unearthed that Conrad's apparent distortions and inventions must be mentioned. See Baines's thorough discussion of the problem in *Conrad: A Critical Biography,* pp. 35–59; esp. pp. 52–53.

28 Gurko, *Joseph Conrad: Giant in Exile,* p. 156.
29 It is perhaps worth remembering in connection with Conrad's pairing of Dominic and Odysseus that Homer's hero comes through his adventures successfully, while Dominic's adventure ends in failure.

CHAPTER 4

1 Blackburn, *Conrad: Letters to Blackwood,* p. 130. Sanchez became Carlos in the published text. Compare Conrad's similar description of his aims in a letter to Pinker from which I quoted in chapter 2: [*Romance*] "is NOT a boy's story . . . the aim being to present the scenes and events and people *strictly realistically* in a glamour of *Romance* . . . a serious attempt at *interesting, animated Romance*" (quoted by Baines, *Conrad: A Critical Biography,* p. 275).
2 Edwin M. Eigner, *Robert Louis Stevenson and Romantic Tradition,* and Robert Kiely, *Robert Louis Stevenson and the Fiction of Adventure.*
3 Geoffrey Hartman, "Romanticism and 'Anti-Self-Consciousness,'" in *Beyond Formalism* (New Haven, 1970), p. 299.
4 M. H. Abrams, "Structure and Style in the Greater Romantic Lyric," in *From Sensibility to Romanticism: Essays Presented to Frederick A. Pottle,* ed. Frederick W. Hilles and Harold Bloom (New York, 1965), pp. 527–60. Poems of this sort, Abrams tells us, "present a determinate speaker in a particularized, and usually a localized, outdoor setting, whom we overhear as he carries on, in a fluent vernacular which rises easily to a more formal speech, a sustained colloquy sometimes with himself or with the outer scene, but more frequently with a silent human auditor" (p. 527). Compare the beginning of *Heart of Darkness,* in which several men seated aboard the cruising yawl *Nellie* are placed in a locale that is rendered with great vividness. One of these men, Marlow, is described with special precision, and he then breaks the silence with a sudden exclamation which introduces a colloquial meditation that rises toward formal speech as easily as the Romantic lyric. "The speaker begins," Abrams continues, describing Marlow as surely as Wordsworth or Coleridge,

with a description of the landscape; an aspect or change of aspect in the landscape evokes a varied but integral process of memory, thought, anticipation, and feeling which remains closely intervolved with the outer scene. In the course of this meditation the lyric speaker achieves an insight, faces up to a tragic loss, comes to a moral decision, or resolves an emotional problem. Often the poem rounds upon itself to end where it began, at the outer scene, but with an altered mood and deepened understanding which is the result of the intervening meditation. [pp. 527–28]

This, surely, is a remarkably complete and accurate description of the essential structure of many of Conrad's first-person pieces, and especially of *Heart of Darkness,* which ends, just as the Romantic lyric does, by rounding upon itself, "at the outer scene, but with an altered mood."

5   This passage from the first chapter of the *Quixote*—I have quoted Walter Starkie's translation (New York, 1964)—seems a convenient distillation of what is perhaps the novel's principal subject as well as the key to its structure.

6   Ian Watt, *The Rise of the Novel* (1957; rpt. Berkeley, Calif., 1959), esp. pp. 9–34.

7   The general argument is summarized in Abrams's essay on the Romantic lyric, cited above in n. 4: "The central enterprise common to many post-Kantian German philosophers and poets, as well as to Coleridge and Wordsworth, was to join together the 'subject' and 'object' that modern intellection had put asunder, and thus to revivify a dead nature, restore its concreteness, significance and human values, and redomiciliate man in a world which had become alien to him. The pervasive sense of estrangement, of a lost and isolated existence in an alien world, is not peculiar to our own age of anxiety, but was a commonplace of Romantic philosophy" (p. 546). Much of Northrop Frye's work argues for the continued dominance of Romantic myths and forms, but see especially the first chapter of his *A Study of English Romanticism* (New

York, 1968). Robert Langbaum's *The Poetry of Experience* (1957; rpt. New York, 1963) is a seminal contribution to the subject, particularly his introduction, "Romanticism as a Modern Tradition," pp. 9–37. Harold Bloom's anthology of essays by various scholars, *Romanticism and Consciousness* (New York, 1970), contains several important papers which show (as Bloom says in a headnote, p. 1) that "subjectivity or self-consciousness is the salient problem of Romanticism, at least for modern readers." Bloom's own *Yeats* (New York, 1970) is full of powerful and unsettling revaluations, many of which challenge the assumption that Romanticism and modernism are discontinuous. Most of Geoffrey Hartman's scholarship is relevant here, but see especially *The Unmediated Vision* (New Haven, 1954) and "Romanticism and 'Anti-Self-Consciousness,'" cited above, n. 3.

8   See, for example, "Pastoral," "A Gossip on a Novel of Dumas's," "A Gossip on Romance," and "A Humble Remonstrance," in *Memories and Portraits, Works* (New York, 1902), vol. 13.

9   Marryat, *Mr. Midshipman Easy* (1836; rpt. London and New York, 1965), p. 27.

10 Jean-Aubry, *Conrad: Life and Letters*, 2: 89.

11 Blackburn, *Conrad: Letters to Blackwood*, p. 133.

12 R. L. Mégroz, *A Talk with Joseph Conrad and a Criticism of His Mind and Method* (London, 1926), p. 71.

13 Garnett, *Letters from Conrad*, pp. 59, 120.

14 Jean-Aubry, *Conrad: Life and Letters*, 1 : 222.

15 Ibid., 1 : 280.

16 My argument here parallels in part that of James Guetti, who sees Marlow's troubled narrative in *Heart of Darkness* as Conrad's way of dramatizing "the failure of imagination" (*The Limits of Metaphor* [Ithaca, N.Y., 1967], pp. 46–68).

17 Laurence Lerner, "Joseph Conrad," in *The Novelist as Innovator*, ed. Walter Allen (London, 1965), p. 84.

18 The letter to Wells is available in *Henry James and H. G. Wells: A Record of Their Friendship . . .* , ed. Leon Edel and Gordon N. Ray (London, 1958), p. 128. The quotations from the preface to *The Ambassadors* are taken from the Scribner's collection of the prefaces, *The Art of*

the Novel, intro. Richard P. Blackmur (New York, 1937), pp. 320, 321.

19 The dreadful candor of Kurtz's last utterance proclaims him to be a "hero of the spirit," according to Lionel Trilling, who interprets *Heart of Darkness* as a parable of "the modern belief about the nature of the artist, the man who goes down into that hell which is the historical beginning of the human soul, a beginning not outgrown but established in humanity as we know it now, preferring the reality of this hell to the bland lies of the civilization that has overlaid it" ("On the Teaching of Modern Literature," in *Beyond Culture* [New York, 1965], pp. 20–21). There is something to this, of course, but I think Trilling may be underestimating Marlow—not to say Conrad. Though he is loyal to Kurtz and sees in him something of what Trilling sees, Marlow also tells us that he is a hollow sham. And it is Marlow himself who is the far more central artist-figure in the novella.

20 *Absalom, Absalom!* (1936; rpt. New York, 1951), p. 251.

21 "To the Reader," in *Quest for Reality: An Anthology of Short Poems in English,* ed. Yvor Winters and Kenneth Fields (Chicago, 1969), p. 168.

22 In *A Personal Record,* p. 15.

23 Guerard, *Conrad the Novelist,* pp. 148–49.

24 Ibid., pp. 154, 153.

25 Ian Watt, "Story and Idea in Conrad's 'The Shadow-Line,'" *Critical Quarterly,* 2 (1960), 145–46.

26 Leslie Fiedler, "The Master of Ballantrae," in *Victorian Literature: Modern Essays in Criticism,* ed. Austin Wright (New York, 1961), pp. 286–87.

27 Blackburn, *Conrad: Letters to Blackwood,* p. 154.

28 Guerard, *Conrad the Novelist,* pp. 40–41.

29 Garnett, *Letters from Conrad,* p. 12.

30 Dennis Donoghue, *The Ordinary Universe: Soundings in Modern Literature* (New York, 1968). Emphasizing what Randall Jarrell calls "the dailiness of life," Donoghue claims for certain modern writers, including late Romantics like Yeats and Rilke, what I am claiming for Conrad. For this antiapocalyptic side of Romanticism, see also Lionel Trilling, "Wordsworth and the Rabbis," in *The Opposing Self* (1955; rpt. New York, 1959), pp. 118–50;

Richard Ellmann's essay on Auden, "Gazebos and Gas-
houses," in *Eminent Domain* (New York, 1967), pp.
97–126; Gordon Haight's introduction to *Adam Bede*
(1948; rpt. New York, 1961), pp. v–xviii, which sees this
side of Wordsworth as the poet's primary legacy in
George Eliot's work; and Karl Kroeber, "The Relevance
and Irrelevance of Romanticism," *Studies in Romanticism,* 9 (1970), 297–306.

31 Hartman, "Wordsworth, Inscriptions and Romantic Nature Poetry," in *Beyond Formalism*, pp. 206–30.

32 Blackburn, *Conrad: Letters to Blackwood*, p. 156.

EPILOGUE

1 Trilling, *The Opposing Self,* pp. 118–50.
2 Originally published in the *Dial,* 75 (1923), 480–83, the
review is accessible in Richard Ellmann and Charles Feidelson, Jr., eds., *The Modern Tradition* (New York,
1965), pp. 679–81.
3 Auerbach, *Mimesis,* trans. Willard R. Trask (Princeton,
1953), p. 551.
4 Irving Howe, *A World More Attractive* (New York,
1963), p. ix.
5 Richard Ellmann, *James Joyce* (1959; rpt. New York,
1965), p. 3.
6 Virginia Woolf, "Modern Fiction," in *The Common
Reader* (1925; rpt. New York, 1953), p. 154.
7 Ford, *Conrad : A Personal Remembrance,* pp. 180–82.
(The spaced periods are in the original; unspaced dots indicate my ellipses.)
8 Ian Watt, "Joseph Conrad: Alienation and Commitment," in *The English Mind,* ed. Hugh Sykes Davies and
George Watson (Cambridge, 1964), p. 275.
9 Philip Rieff, *Freud: The Mind of the Moralist* (New
York, 1959); Lionel Trilling, "Freud and Literature," in
The Liberal Imagination (1950; rpt. New York, 1957),
pp. 32–54; and "Freud: Within and Beyond Culture," in
Beyond Culture, pp. 89–118.
10 Trans. W. D. Robson-Scott (1953; rpt. New York, 1957),
p. 88.
11 Walter Allen, ed., *The Novelist as Innovator* (London,
1965), Introduction, p. xii.

12 Stevenson, "A Gossip on Romance," *Memories and Portraits, Works* (New York, 1902), 13 : 329.
13 Ford, *Return to Yesterday*, p. 217.
14 Lionel Trilling, *A Gathering of Fugitives* (New York, 1957), p. 41.
15 *Return to Yesterday*, p. 212. Ford also tells us that James called Marlow "that preposterous master mariner" (*Conrad: A Personal Remembrance*, p. 161).
16 Jean-Aubry, *Conrad: Life and Letters*, 2 : 55, 91.
17 *The Shadow-Line*, p. 108. The quoted phrase in the next paragraph is from the "Familiar Preface" to *A Personal Record*, p. xxi.

Index

Abrams, M. H.: on greater Romantic lyric, 103, 189*n*4; on Romanticism and modernism, 106, 190*n*7

Academy: reviews *Typhoon,* 6–7

Adventure story: as Romantic mode, 4, 100–03, 106–08; Conrad's reliance on conventions of, 5–11, 41–60; Conrad's affinities for, 13–23; popularity of in 1890s and after, 24–25, 171*nn*1,3, 172*n*10; hero and retainer in, 43–44; as *bildungsroman,* 43–56; *Lord Jim* as, 53–56, 93, 130–37, 141, 145; Stevenson on, 54, 162; elements of in *The Mirror of the Sea,* 87–99, 135, 141; first-person narrators in, 101–02, 120–21; "Youth" as, 135–37, 142; *Heart of Darkness* as, 135–46; *The Shadow-Line* as, 136–40, 146; "The Secret Sharer" as, 140–46; plot conventions of, and Conrad, 145–46. *See also* Faithful retainer

Aldington, Richard, 154

Allen, Walter, 162

Almayer's Folly (1895), 24, 40, 63–65 passim; early reviews of, 3, 7–10, 168*n*5, 169*n*17; Conrad on writing of, 66–67, 74–76

Arrow of Gold, The (1919), 19; compared to *Romance,* 38–39; Dominic Cervoni in, 46–48, 50

Athenaeum: reviews *Typhoon,* 5–6; reviews *Lord Jim,* 8; eulogizes Stevenson, 24–25; reviews *Romance,* 172*n*10

Aubry. *See* Jean-Aubry, G.

Auden, W. H., 150; "In Memory of W. B. Yeats," 126

Auerbach, Erich, 154–55

Baines, Jocelyn, 19, 78

Barth, John, 105

Beckett, Samuel, 127

Blackwood, William: Conrad's letters to, 13, 28, 30, 100–01, 109–10, 142, 148

Blackwood's Edinburgh Magazine, 85

Blake, William, xii, 4

Bloom, Harold, xii, 106, 191*n*7

Borges, Jorge Luis, 105

Brontë, Charlotte: *Jane Eyre,* 120

Castro, Thomas (in *Romance*): as faithful retainer, 44–46, 48, 49, 139, 141–42

Cervantes, Miguel de: *Don Quixote,* 105–06

Cervoni, Dominic (in *The Mirror of the Sea* and *The Arrow of Gold*), 107; as prototype of Conrad's faithful retainers, 46–53, 59, 96, 129–30, 132, 141–42; role in *The Mirror,* 93–99

Chance (1913), 13, 21, 37, 57; narrator in, 103–05

Clifford, Sir Hugh: Conrad letter to, 112–13; *In a Corner of Asia* (1899), 112

Coleridge, Samuel Taylor: preface to "Kubla Khan" and Conrad, 127; "Dejection: An Ode," 129; "To William Wordsworth," 129

Colvin, Sir Sidney, 19